AF867774

What to Automate,
What to Keep Human, and
Where the Real ROI is in
Game Production

The AI Game Plan

Mathieu F. Lachance

CONTENTS

> *AI is not going to replace humans, but humans with AI are going to replace humans without AI.*

—Karim Lakhani

Harvard Business School professor, Workplace technology

Co-Author, Competing in the Age of AI:

Strategy and Leadership When Algorithms and Networks Run the World

1 ACKNOWLEDGMENTS

First and foremost, I'd like to deeply thank my beautiful wife, Audrey, and my two boisterous boys, James and Logan. You've been incredibly patient with me, and your encouragement throughout this journey was the anchor I needed during the challenging moments of these last few years.

I would also like to thank my former bosses, Igor Efremov, Sonia Sedler, Jon Hauck, and Bertrand Bodson, who welcomed and supported my entry into and progress in the Executive MBA program, which ultimately led to this research and book. Your belief in my potential has been instrumental to my success.

I would like to thank my Master's Program Directors, Louis Hébert and Alain Pinsonneault, and my research supervisor, Taha Havakhor, for their ongoing guidance throughout my studies. Alain and Louis, thank you for forcing me to find a less theoretical, more practical research subject. Taha, your understanding of academia and passion for technology, as well as your challenge to my data interpretation, really allowed me to find the diamonds in the rough.

Last but not least, I'd like to thank everyone who shared their time and knowledge through interviews and "that was way more than 15 minutes" conference coffee breaks! Your insights have been priceless and genuinely enriched my understanding of the subject matter.

2 PREFACE

This book, and the research it represents, is the culmination of my academic efforts and, more importantly, a personal journey of growth and discovery. Over the past 3 years, I have researched, discussed, and reflected on AI, both in general and in the context of video game development. This has broadened my view on its uses, efficiency gains, and productivity. I am excited to share my findings and insights through this work.

Thank you to everyone who has been part of this journey. Your contributions have made this achievement possible.

Notes to the reader

This book is a mostly direct transcription of my Master's research paper. It doesn't read like a book, and you likely shouldn't read it like one, as it may make for a very boring read. The most important and valuable parts of the book are the practical AI application (Section 6) and the overall results (Section 7). Some sections may not be of interest to you, such as the methodology (Section 5) and research limitations (Section 8). I included them anyway for anyone who might be curious.

The practical applications in Section 6 are divided into the six pre-production and production game development services: design, engineering, visual arts, audio, quality assurance, and localization. Each service is further subdivided into subsections and tool applications where applicable. I have not included videogame post-production AI research and application, such as marketing, customer support, or distribution.

Section 7 is split into two subsections. The first one tallies the results of the research itself, and the second covers the key learnings. The key learnings are the interesting insights I've gained through research, expert consultations, and interpreting the quantifiable data to understand their implications for the broader game industry and its stakeholders.

The AI tools evaluated in this research were assessed based on their capabilities and performance until 2025. Please be aware that AI has progressed rapidly and advanced in both game development and other fields since this research was completed and published.

All currency amounts referenced in this book are presented in United States dollars (USD) for simplicity, standardization, and clarity. This approach aims to ease readers' understanding and ensure consistency throughout the book.

The terms cost savings, cost efficiency, and cost effectiveness are used interchangeably throughout the research. In the context of this research, they all refer to the same concept: the potential cost reduction amount ($) or proportion (%) resulting from leveraging AI positively in videogame production.

3 EXECUTIVE SUMMARY

This research examines the practical application, cost-saving opportunities, and potential productivity gains of artificial intelligence in video game development.

Key findings include:

1. The study encompasses a diverse range of AI applications in **Game Design, Engineering, Visual Art, Audio Creation, Quality Assurance, and Localization**.
2. Implementing AI in game development can significantly boost productivity. **AI-assisted processes produce 76% more output overall** for the same costs as traditional human-only approaches. Some specific AI applications can deliver productivity gains of over 1,000%.
3. The research demonstrates substantial cost savings through AI adoption. **AI-supported processes can cut game development costs by an average of 43% compared to traditional methods**. Some specific AI applications achieve savings of over 90%.
4. The research demonstrates **current and potential disruptions in B2C game product markets, B2B game publishing, B2B outsourcing services, and in the AI industry as a whole.**

This research examines the impact of AI on game development, both currently and in the future. It offers insights for industry professionals and researchers. It underscores AI's transformative potential in gaming.

> *"Quand on parle d'AI, le but, c'est la productivité. Ce n'est pas la créativité."*
>
> *AI translation: "When we talk about AI, the goal is productivity, not creativity."*
>
> —Interview with Pierre-Paul Giroux
> Vice-President Engineering A.I. at Unity

4 Introduction

As of 2023, GPT outperformed 75% of Medical College Admission Test (MCAT) takers, 88% of Law School Admission Test (LSAT) takers, and 90% of Bar exam takers. It surpassed most Advanced Placement (AP) students, usually scoring around the 90th percentile in most courses. [1,2]

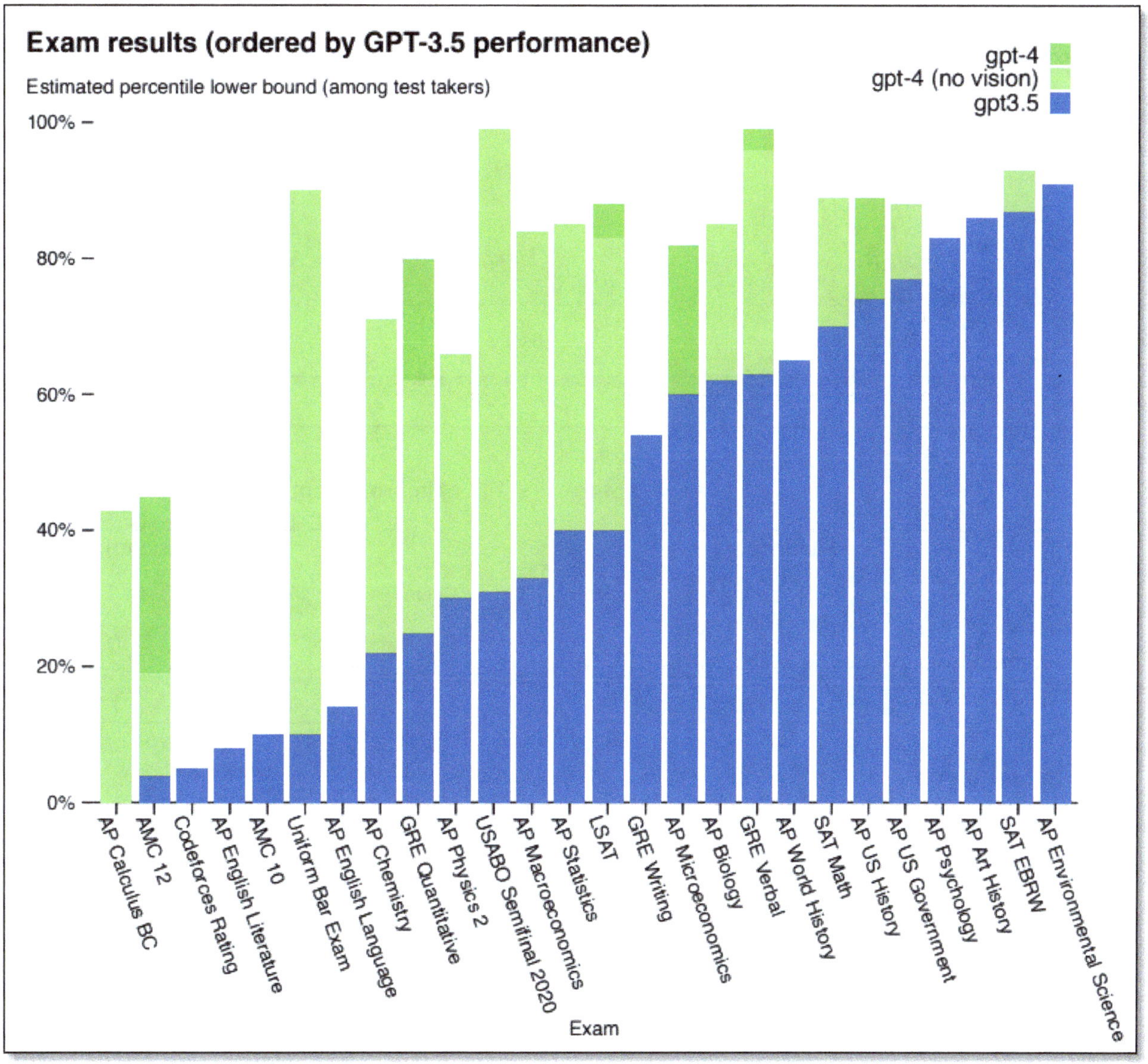

[1] GPT-4 Technical Report, OpenAI, https://cdn.openai.com/papers/gpt-4.pdf, 27 March 2023

[2] Advanced Placement (AP) is a program in the US and Canada that offers undergraduate university-level courses and examinations to high school students.

As of September 2024, OpenAI o1 now ranks in the 89th percentile on competitive programming questions (Codeforces). It ranks among the top 500 USA Math Olympiad (AIME) students. It exceeds average expert-level human PhD-level accuracy on physics, biology, and chemistry problems (GPQA).[3]

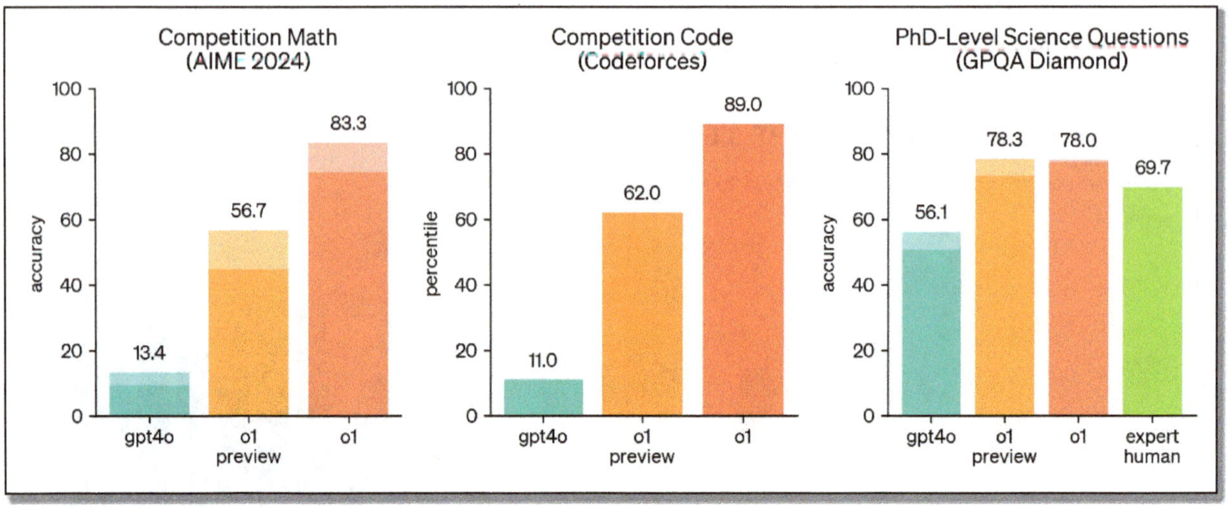

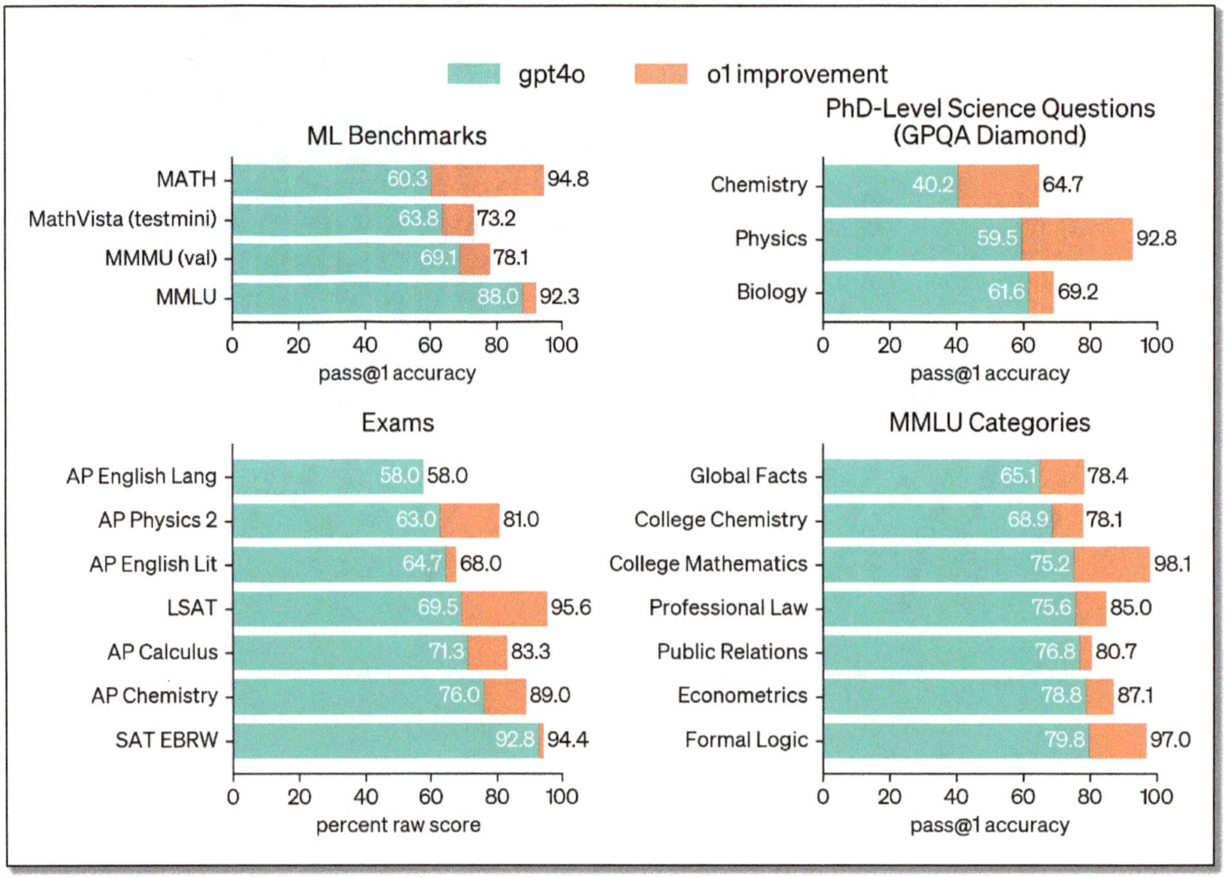

[3] Learning to Reason with LLMs, OpenAI, https://openai.com/index/learning-to-reason-with-llms/, 12 September 2024

An analysis by Goldman Sachs Research's economists predicts that two-thirds of the approximately 900 current U.S. professions could be partially automated by AI. These professions involve repetitive, rule-based tasks that can be performed more efficiently by artificial intelligence. The researchers also estimate that 25 to 50% of those affected positions could be replaced soon. The researchers note that, while significant, most jobs are only partly exposed to AI automation. This means that many jobs may be supplemented by AI, rather than replaced. [4]

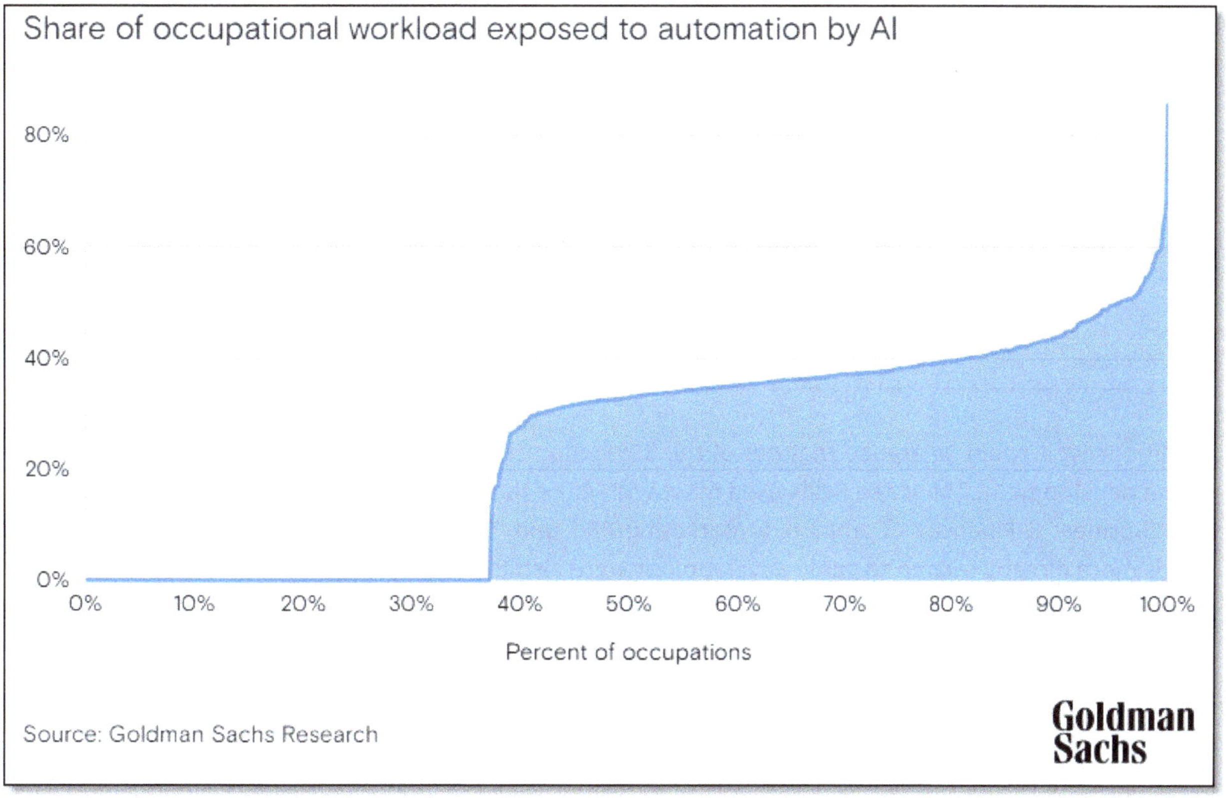

In the fast-paced, competitive world of game development, AI is a game-changer and a beacon of hope for game executives. The post-pandemic video game slowdown has put pressure on budgets, but the rise of AI as a key tool offers hope for the industry.[5] Integrating AI into game development is now a reality, not a dream. Thus, embracing AI is not just a strategic choice but a necessity for staying competitive in this rapidly evolving industry.

AI is a hot topic in media and game industry discussions. Yet, there's a lack of analysis on its impact on the video game development pipeline. This gap in understanding underscores the need for more research and exploration in this area.

---

[4]Generative AI could raise global GDP by 7%, Goldman Sachs, https://www.goldmansachs.com/intelligence/pages/generative-ai-could-raise-global-gdp-by-7-percent.html, 5 April 2023

[5]2023–2024 video game industry layoffs, Wikipedia, https://en.wikipedia.org/wiki/2023%E2%80%932024_video_game_industry_layoffs , visited 14 July 2024

Despite its visibility and potential benefits, most game development professionals aren't yet using generative AI tools. Per 3,000 people surveyed through the GDC State of the Game Industry 2023 report, only 31% of respondents advised using an AI tool of some sort for their work[6].

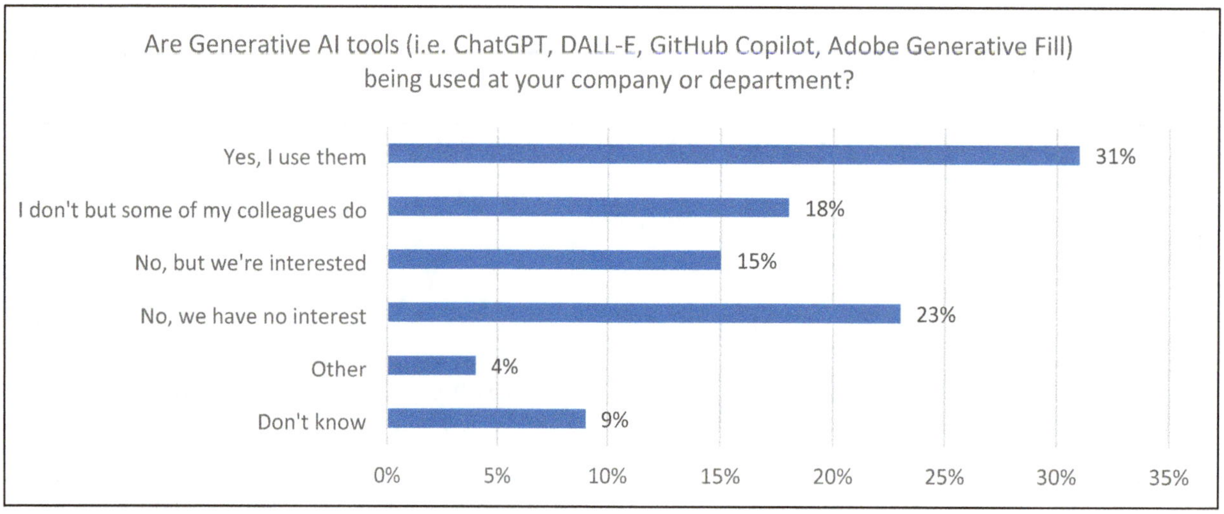

Additionally, it could be argued that out of the 31% who use it, most use it for tasks unrelated to direct game development. The three fields used most with AI by the surveyed people who answered positively are "Business & Finance," "Community/Marketing/PR," and "Production & Team Management." The six fields more directly related to game development were also the least AI-applied.

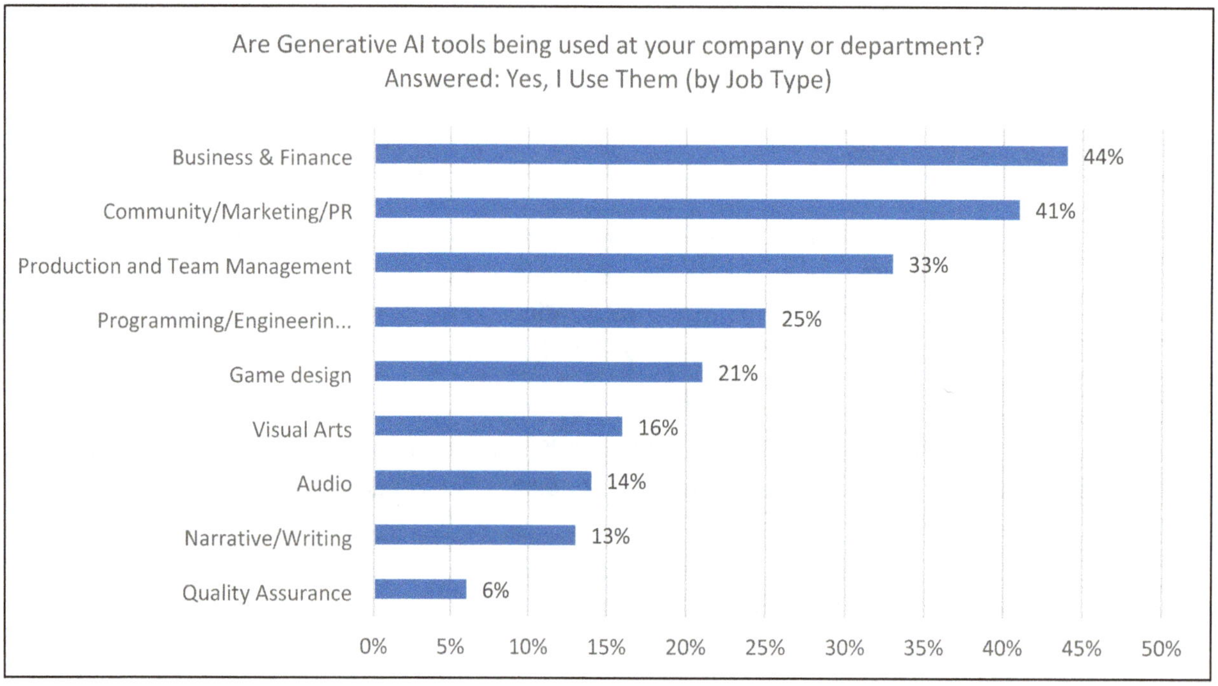

[6] GDC State of the Game Industry 2023 report, GDC, https://reg.gdconf.com/state-of-game-industry-2024, January 2024

Additionally, although larger studios would likely benefit more from incorporating AI into their development pipelines, considering the size of their games, teams, and budgets, indie studios outpace their larger counterparts in AI adoption.

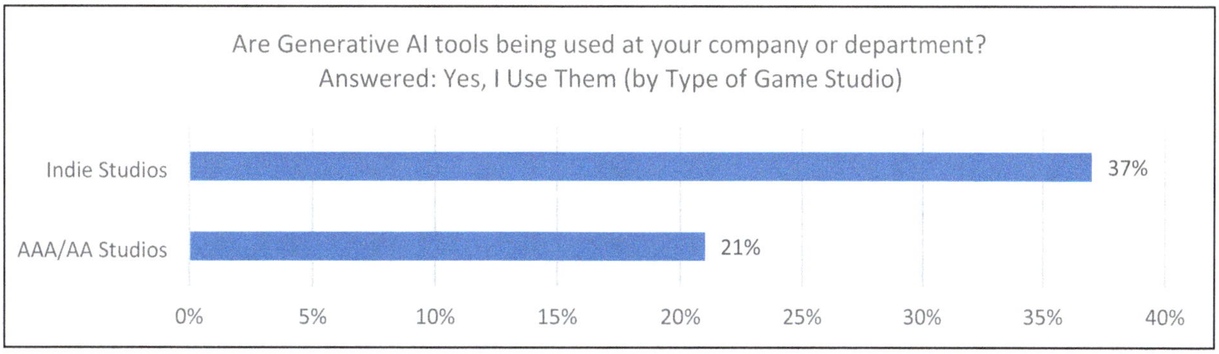

Potentially due to legal or ethical repercussions, 21% of surveyed AAA developers reported that their company had outright banned such tools, compared to 9% of indie developers. While developers may have doubts regarding the industry implications of Generative AI, they are convinced about its ethical impact. Most developers (84%) reported being either somewhat or very concerned about the ethics of applying generative artificial intelligence. Concerns include AI bias, job displacement, and the dissemination of harmful content. 12% were not concerned.

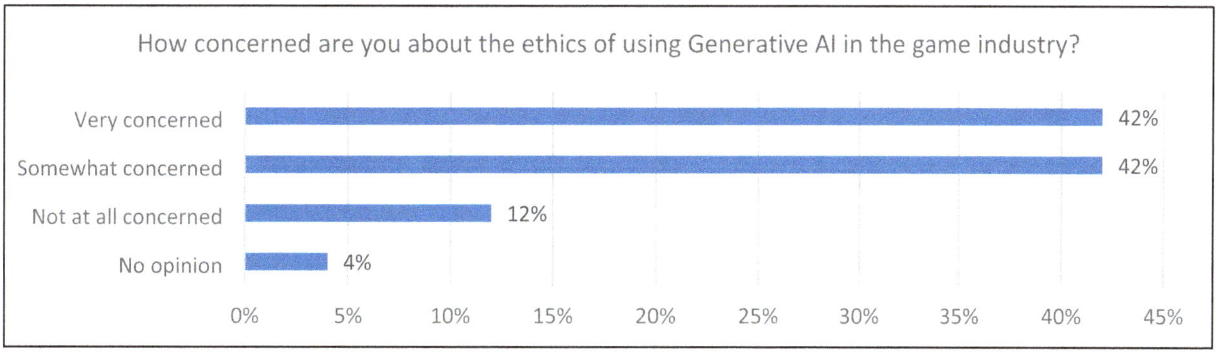

In this research, I aim to explain how AI technology can automate game development processes and quantify potential productivity gains and cost savings. To achieve this objective, I took a multifaceted approach. It included a thorough review of existing literature, interviews with industry experts, and self-experimentation. I also examined case studies from game developers, AI tool providers, consulting firms, investment firms, and think tanks.

This book delves into the diverse applications of AI across various stages of game development, including:

1. **Game Design & Story:** AI-assisted design tools that streamline creative processes.

2. **Game Development:** AI-powered code generation.

3. **Art Creation:** Automated generation of assets, characters, and environments.

4. **Audio Creation:** AI-driven music composition, sound effects generation, and voiceovers.

5. **Quality Assurance:** AI-driven testing and bug detection.

6. **Localization:** AI-driven translation and voiceover processes.

I present a summary of my findings as an outcome. It reveals a compelling story of AI-driven changes in the game development industry. I show these findings as quantifiable reductions in production costs and increases in production outputs.

> *"When GDC surveys say that 90 percent of developers have used generative AI, what most people mean is that they've used ChatGPT in some capacity."*
>
> —Interview with Stephen Peacock
> Director AI at 2K, Ex-Head of AI at AWS & Keywords

5 Methodology

5.1 Research Question

Our primary research question is:

- Within the video game development process, which steps can be automated fully or partially with the use of AI, and what are the associated productivity gains and cost savings for each of those steps, where applicable?

This question can be further split into:

- What are the different game development services within the video game development process?
- What are the different game development sub-disciplines per service?
- For each different game development sub-discipline identified,
    - Where has AI been, or where can it be applied to automate manual human work?
    - What are the current and potential work AI automation cost savings?
    - What are the current and potential work AI automation productivity gains?

5.2 Measurement

In this paper, I define cost savings as the amount by which less is needed to generate a similar quality output on the same project when AI is leveraged positively. Mathematically, it can be represented as

Cost saving = Human-only cost – AI-supplemented cost

where

AI-supplemented cost = AI-supplemented Human cost + AI-supplemented Machine cost

Visually and on a % ratio, it can be represented as

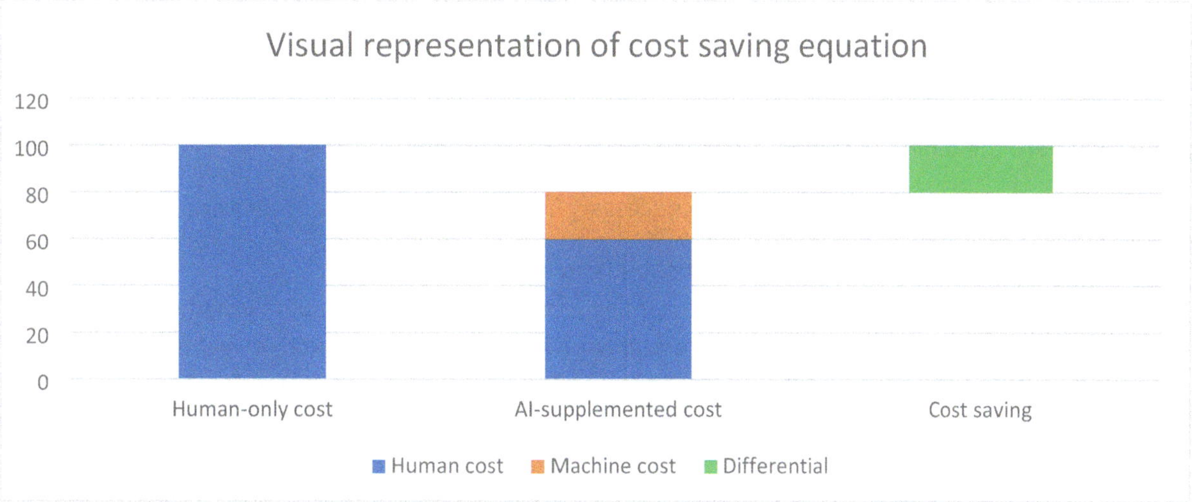

Note that I use the terms cost savings, cost efficiency, and cost effectiveness interchangeably throughout the research. In the context of this research, all refer to the same concept: the potential cost reduction amount ($) or proportion (%) resulting from leveraging AI positively.

I define productivity gains as the increased output of a similar quality generated on the same project when AI is leveraged positively. Mathematically, it can be represented as

Productivity gain = AI-supplemented output - Human-only output

where

AI-supplemented output = AI-supplemented Human output + AI-supplemented Machine output

Visually and on a % ratio, it can be represented as

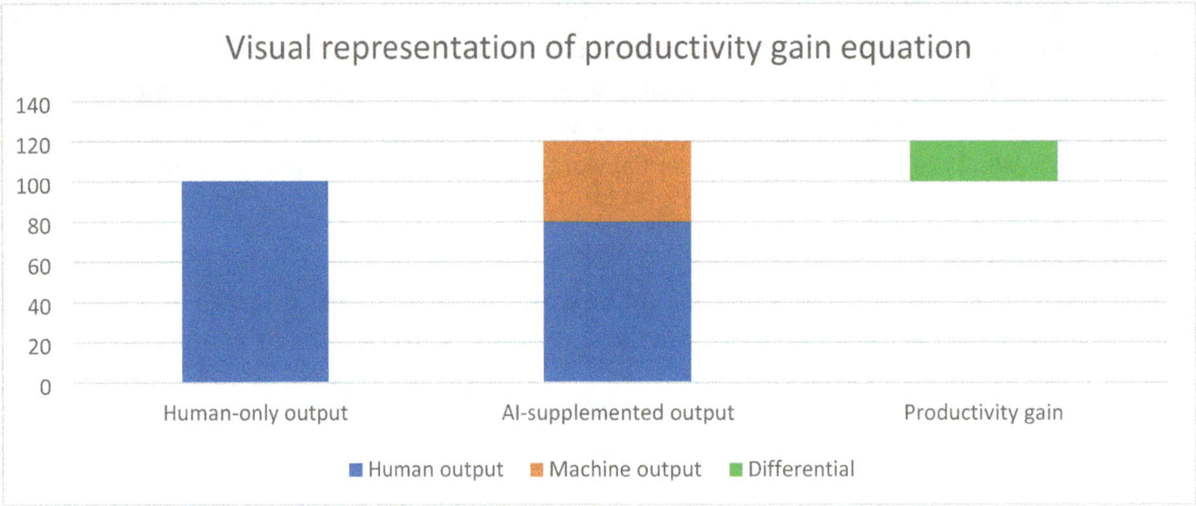

5.3 Strategy

Out of the above research questions, I have used literature and other information available to generate these questions:

- What are the different game development services within the video game development process?
- What are the different game development sub-disciplines per service?

I've used field expert interviews to gather the necessary information to answer these questions:

- For each different game development sub-discipline identified,
  - Where does AI have or can be applied to automate some manual human work?
  - What are the current and potential work AI automation productivity gains?
  - What are the current and potential work AI automation cost savings?

This enables me to gather all the necessary, quantifiable information related to my research question.

In addition to the above, I've also gathered qualitative information from those same field experts. I've asked them to comment on any unquantifiable gains from developing or applying AI technology to their game development fields.

5.4 Scope

To obtain an average market result, in most cases, we've opted to base our analysis on examples of large, high-end 3D AA games with development budgets of $10 million. In some cases, we've extended the study to a few other types of games and budget sizes, allowing us to review a broader range of tools.

The videogame market is large, with an estimated projected global revenue of 282.3$ billion on the B2C side for 2024.[7] Games range from small indie games to large AAA. The exact scope definitions of Indie, AA, and AAA differ among experts, especially when discussing budget sizes. In this research, we've used the below as a basic rule.

Game Type	Indie	AA	AAA
Development Budget	Less than $1M	$1M-50M	$50M+

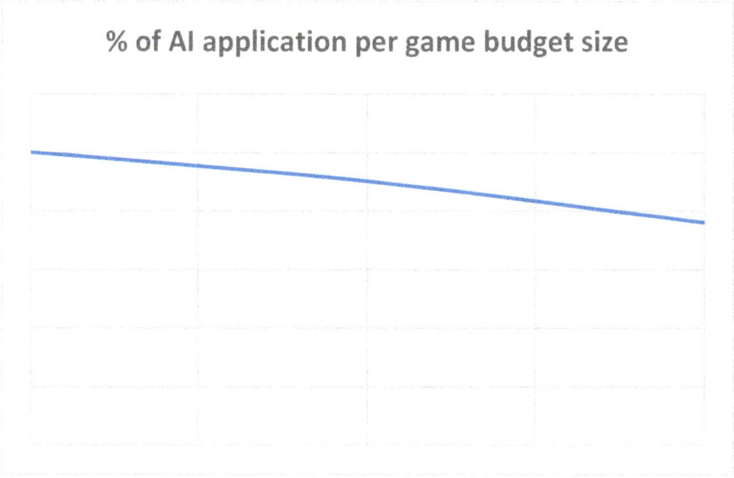

Despite the large range, most AA games have a budget of less than $10 million. We've used $10 million as a benchmark to cover a proper market average.

Apart from effectiveness's sake, we've used this average scope to also gather more accurate results, with the assumption that AI applications are more widespread in Indie games than in AAA games, with AA being a middle ground sweet spot, as seen in the introduction.

5.5 Sources

5.5.1 Literature review

The literature review examines existing research and case studies on AI in game development, as well as relevant work outside of game development in adjacent markets, such as media and entertainment. This section covers findings from different sources, including academic journals, industry reports, and self-published case studies from top game companies. Industry applications display AI's evolving role. By examining current applications, this research demonstrates how theory translates into practical AI innovations. It maps the growing landscape of artificial intelligence.

The review identified diverse applications of AI across all stages of game development, revealing several key themes. It highlighted significant productivity gains and cost savings possibilities attributed to AI applications.

[7] Market insights Video Games – Worldwide, Statista, https://www.statista.com/outlook/dmo/digital-media/video-games/worldwide, March 2024

The literature also uncovers a significant gap in AI game development workflow analyses. Many articles discuss theories or provide high-level overviews. Few, however, examine practical implementations and outcomes in detail. This gap highlights the need for additional real-world research in this area.

Case studies from industry leaders provided concrete examples of successful AI integration strategies. These case studies illustrate the benefits and challenges faced during implementation, including change resistance and workforce displacement solutions.

The literature review provided a solid foundation for understanding the current state of AI in game development and identified areas that require further investigation.

5.5.2 Expert interviews

This research is based on a series of expert interviews with professionals from various sectors of the video game industry. The interviews aimed to gather insights on the practical applications of artificial intelligence (AI) in game development. Participants included game designers, engineers, artists, and audio, localization, and QA specialists. Each had a unique perspective on how AI is reshaping their field.

The structured interview format facilitated the exploration of key AI themes. Interviewees were asked to describe their roles and expertise, providing context for their insights into AI applications. Questions focused on identifying areas where AI can automate tasks and explaining current and potential applications. Participants shared data on current AI applications. They cited percentages highlighting significant reductions in production time and cost, and advised on the unexpected benefits of AI integration. For example, several interviewees noted that AI tools improved creativity and teamwork.

The expert interviews provided rich qualitative and quantitative data, forming a critical part of the key findings. The insights gained validated existing literature and illuminated new avenues for future research into the role of AI in game development.

The following are the standard interview questions that were used.

- Can you briefly describe your position and the company you work for? (anonymize or pseudonymize if needed)
- Can you provide a short description or list of your field(s) of expertise in video game development, if applicable? (e.g., 2D art assets, Game development for racing games, Game porting from PC to Console for 4x strategy games, QA, Localization, Voice-overs, etc.)
- Can you describe your field of expertise in AI video game development, if applicable? (e.g., application of AI into audio localization pipelines, generative AI art, buying AI services, etc.)
- Are you working at a company offering those AI services/products?
    - If so, what AI are you applying/developing to your solutions? Why?
- For each different game development field you have expertise in,
    - Where can we apply AI to automate some manual human work?
    - What are the current work AI automation cost savings? (in time or cost % savings)
    - What are the potential work AI automation cost savings? (in time or cost % savings)
    - What are the current work AI automation productivity gains? (in time or asset % output)
    - What are the potential productivity gains from AI automation? (in time or asset % output)
- From your point of view, are there any qualitative gains from using AI in game development?

- Have you had any surprises either applying or developing AI for game development? If so, what are they?
- Anything else you think I should be aware of that we haven't discussed?

5.5.3 Self-experimentation

The self-experimentation component involved hands-on work with various game development AI tools. This hands-on approach helped me better understand how to apply these technologies at different stages of game production.

Throughout this phase, I have tested several leading AI tools for content generation, asset adaptation, and more. When applicable, I evaluated each tool based on its effectiveness in automating specific aspects of game development.

This step highlighted the impact of AI on game development workflows and supported findings from expert interviews and literature reviews. This mix of theory and practice deepened my understanding and gave me a well-rounded view of AI's transformative role in this fast-changing industry.

6 Application

6.1 Game design

Game design is the foundation of video game development. The first step in creating a video game involves all the ideation, organization, and planning that go into making the final interactive experience. It includes several key aspects:

- Core concept development (brainstorming, ideation, game genre)
- Game mechanics and systems design (fundamental gameplay, target audience)
- Narrative and world design (scenes, screenplay, environment)
- Documentation and communication (Game Design Documents)

Using an average game project for evaluation, the analysis shows a 91.9% cost efficiency gain from using AI-assisted platforms. Note that AI-supplemented savings were evaluated conservatively. So, the variance between human-only and AI-supplemented costs may exceed the value reported below, which is already high. This conservative evaluation was conducted to minimize bias, enhance the relative value of the data, and increase trust in the data itself.

"I use it for ideation, but I use it carefully because it's like a rubber duck where you just talk to it to flesh out your ideas. You have to be careful because the ideas it gives you back might not be exactly what you're looking for. And you have to make sure it doesn't bias you into something that might not be as good as what you could do without it."

—Interview with Dylan Ebert, PhD
Developer Advocate Engineer, Hugging Face

Applying AI reduces human costs to 7.5% of previous human-only estimates, and the AI tool supports this at a cost of 0.6% of those same original estimates, totaling 8.1% of the original price.

Game design costs	Human-only cost	AI-supplemented cost		Variation
		Human	AI[8]	
Core concept	$2,000	$100	$0.01	-95.0%
Mechanics	$2,000	$100	$0.01	-95.0%
Concept art	$10,000	$400	$120	-94.8%
Storyboard	$2,000	$100	$0.01	-95.0%
Script	$2,000	$400	$0.02	-80.0%
GDD	$2,000	$400	$0.01	-80.0%
Total	**$20,000**	**$1,500**	**$120.04**	**-91.9%**
Total	**$20,000**	**$1,620.04**		**-91.9%**

[8] Where $0.01 appears, the actual cost is a fraction of $0.01, rounded up.

Total %	**100%**	**7.5%**	**0.6%**	**-91.9%**

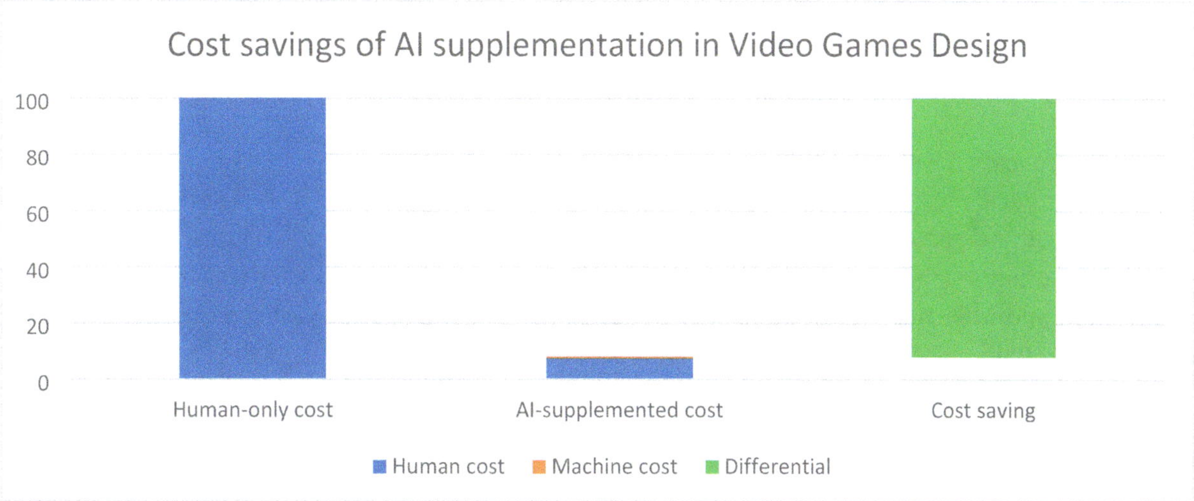

From these cost calculations, we can extrapolate an output that is ≈approximately 12 times greater with AI supplementation, resulting in a productivity gain of 1,134.54%.

Game design output	Human-only output	AI-supplemented output
Output	1	12.3454
Productivity gains		**1,134.54%**

Game design output	Human-only Human cost & output	AI-supplemented Human cost & output	AI-supplemented Machine cost	AI-supplemented Machine output
Value 1	$20,000	$1,500	$120.04	$18,500
Ratio 1	100%	7.5%	0.6%	92.5%
Ratio AI-sup	1,234.5%	**92.6%**	7.4%	**1,141.9%**

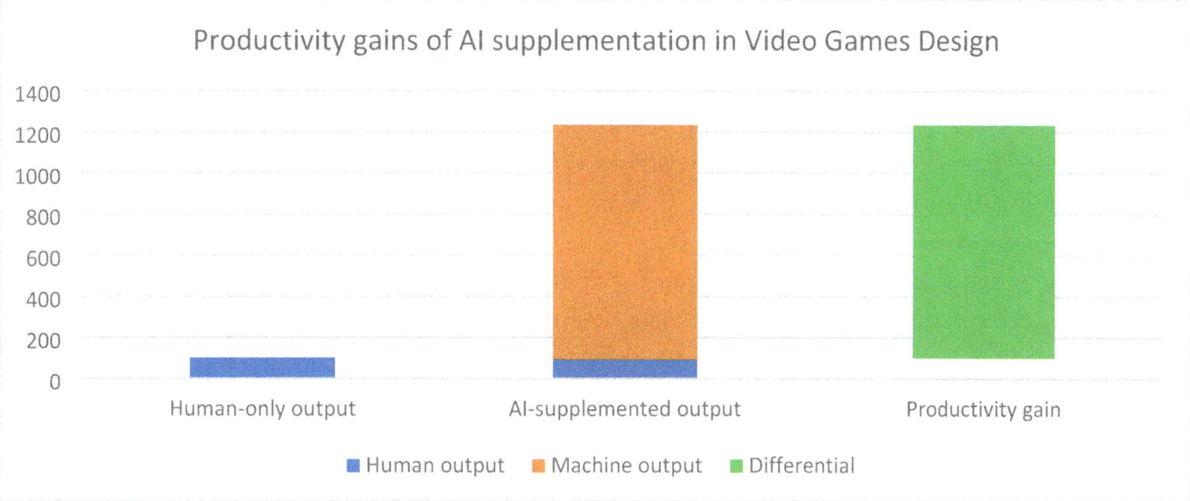

As addressed in the following sub-sections, these numbers are conservative. AI ratios were usually chosen because they are limited not by the platforms themselves but by how humans need to interact with them. Removing these limitations, where possible, could increase productivity gains a thousandfold or more.

Note that one tool, unmentioned in the following subsections, Ludo.ai, offers features that cover most of the game design phases. It also offers automated market feedback, which they call *Ludo score.* [9]

6.1.1 Core concept development

While humans decide what the game is, how to play it, and how to structure it, AI can drastically speed up work output and reduce prototyping and ideation times. At this stage, a Producer, ideation team, marketing, or other team(s) usually brainstorm ideas based on existing or new licenses, target audiences, market data, and objectives. Teams select the most promising concept(s) based on multiple criteria, including potential fun, originality, feasibility, and return on investment.

Experiential trials of these tools show that AI can generate more, and often better, ideas faster than most pre-existing human teams. Here's a brief experiment with Gemini, featuring an output generated from the first prompt, that could easily challenge some of the best ideation and marketing teams out there. The prompt and ideation output took less than 20 seconds and can be iterated and adjusted endlessly, based on market data and objectives, with minimal to no additional cost.

Prompt into Google's Gemini: *"Gemini, please generate 10 videogame ideas starring Adam Sandler as the main character."*

Output: *"**10 Video Game Ideas Starring Adam Sandler***

Comedy-Focused Games

1. ***Sandy's Sandwich Shop Simulator:*** *Adam plays a hapless sandwich shop owner who must learn to balance absurd customer demands, food safety regulations, and the occasional alien invasion.*
2. ***The Waterboy: Gridiron Glory:*** *A sequel to the classic movie, this game focuses on Bobby Boucher's journey to becoming a legendary football coach, complete with hilarious sideline antics and motivational speeches.*
3. ***Happy Gilmore: Golfing Through Life:*** *A golf-based life simulator where players follow Happy Gilmore's journey from hockey enforcer to golf prodigy, facing off against rival golfers and eccentric course designs.*
4. ***Billy Madison: Back to School:*** *A platformer where players guide Billy Madison through his academic challenges, facing off against bullies, teachers, and the occasional talking animal.*
5. ***Little Nicky: Demon Delivery Service:*** *A comedic action-adventure where Adam plays Nicky, a reluctant demon who must deliver souls while dealing with his mischievous brothers and the challenges of the underworld.*

Action-Adventure Games

6. ***The Wedding Singer: Rock Star Rampage:*** *A rhythm-action game where Adam plays Robbie Hart, a struggling wedding singer who must use his musical talents to defeat rival bands and save the day.*
7. ***Click: Time-Traveling Troubleshooter:*** *A time-traveling adventure where Adam plays Michael Newman, a man who can control time and must fix historical blunders caused by his younger self.*

[9] Create hit games with the power of AI, Ludo.ai, https://ludo.ai/, visited July 2024

8. ***You Don't Mess with the Zohan: Counter-Terrorist Commando:*** *An over-the-top action game where Adam plays Zohan, a former Israeli counter-terrorist turned hair stylist, who must use his combat skills to save New York City.*
9. ***Reign Over Me:*** *A character-driven adventure where Adam plays Charlie Fineman, a man struggling to cope with loss. Players must guide him through his journey of grief and healing, with a focus on emotional storytelling.*
10. ***Punch-Drunk Love:*** *A boxing simulator with a comedic twist, where Adam plays Barry Egan, a lonely businessman who discovers his inner fighter. Players must train Barry to become a boxing champion while managing his quirky family and love life.*

Would you like to develop one of these ideas further, or do you have another character in mind?"

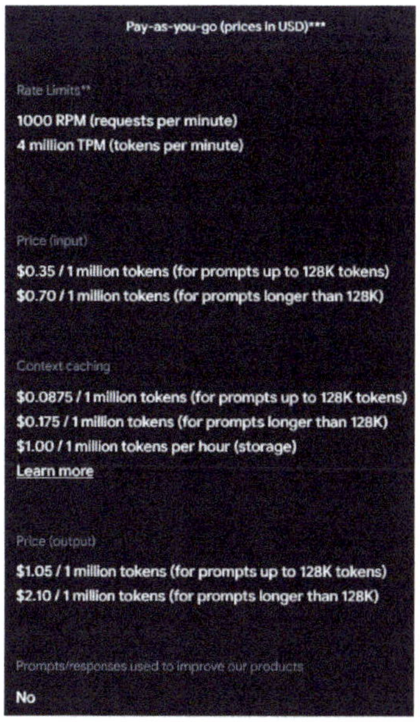

A quality output of this level would have historically required the research and application of a team of several experienced individuals over the course of a week's work. These ideas were generated in under a minute using AI.

Gemini's price point is free if you wish for your content and prompts to be used to improve the platform, and thus used freely by Google. Assuming that a game developer or publisher would want to keep this information private, the above example would have cost 6/100th of a cent through Gemini's *Pay-as-you-go* model.[10]

Assuming 1 week's worth of human-only work at $50/hour and a conservative AI-supplemented 2 hours of work instead of the "less than a minute" result we got from our self-experiment; it would still generate a 95% cost efficiency.

Gemini cost PAYG	Character length	Gemini Tokens	Cost per 1M token	Total cost
Input	86	21.5	$0.35	$0.0000077
Output	2264	566	$1.05	$0.0005943
Total				**$0.000602**

Core concept cost	Human-only cost	AI-supplemented cost	Variation
Human cost	$2000	$100	-95%
AI/Tool cost	$0	$0.000602	
Total	**$2000**	**$100.000602**	**-95%**

Even when paid, the price of the AI service is so insignificant that it has no significant impact on the overall cost. Additionally, the potential productivity improvement would be limited only by human factors and time when using AI platforms. Using the example above, a person or team of people could easily generate 20 of these concepts using AI within a week, likely many more. They would have equal or better quality, and the time required would match that of generating just one normally.

[10] Gemini API Pricing, Google, https://ai.google.dev/pricing, 31 July 2024

Furthermore, generating these ideas every 2 minutes instead of once per week would mean being 1,200 times more efficient. Using tools to "batch" these or requesting the machine to develop these concepts over a week, every 2 minutes, would mean being 5,040 times more efficient. By batching these and asking the AI to creatively craft the prompts, while allowing a more realistic output time of 20 seconds, the efficiency would increase to 30,240 times.

Core concept productivity	Human-only output	AI-supplemented output	Variation
Core concept generation per cost efficiency calculation (40h)	1	20	+1900%
Core concept generation in 1 week – unbatched 2m (40h)	1	1200	+119 900%
Core concept generation in 1 week - batched 2m (168h)	1	5040	+503 900%
Core concept generation in 1 week - batched 20s (168h)	1	30 240	+3 023 900%

Again, human factors would limit all of these, so take it with a grain of salt. An efficient prompt engineer with a proper AI platform should be able to attain these latter types of results after a few iterations. At that point, limitations only come from people who need to review these outputs. Even then, an algorithm and prompt could be set in place to ask an AI, based on limiting factors (such as market and audience), which core designs are most likely to succeed given the specified criteria. That limitation would be significantly reduced, provided that the average output of that query is trusted and accurate.

6.1.2 Game mechanics and system design

Once developers turn base ideas into applicable concepts, they develop core game mechanics and system designs to support them. Here, AI also seems to excel. It can match or outperform human teams that manually create this content or try to generate those ideas. Note that the following prompt also generated an unrequested experience design essential to the overarching game design.

Follow-up prompt into Google's Gemini: "Thanks, Gemini. Can you take the first game and develop and explain the core game mechanics to be applied, and the system design, please?"

Output: "**Sandy's Sandwich Shop Simulator**

Core Game Mechanics

- **Order Management:** Players must efficiently handle incoming orders, juggling multiple requests simultaneously. This involves selecting the correct ingredients, assembling sandwiches, and packaging them for delivery.
- **Customer Satisfaction:** Players need to balance speed and accuracy to satisfy customers. Satisfied customers will return and tip generously, while dissatisfied customers will leave negative reviews.
- **Inventory Management:** Maintaining sufficient supplies of bread, meats, cheeses, and other ingredients is crucial. Players must order new stock to avoid running out.
- **Time Management:** The game should introduce increasing pressure as the day progresses, with more orders and time constraints.
- **Upgrading:** Players can earn money to upgrade their shop equipment (faster toasters, slicers, etc.) and expand their menu.

- **Mini-games:** To add variety and challenge, mini-games could be introduced, such as slicing meat perfectly or correctly identifying ingredients.

System Design

Core Loop:

1. **Order Reception:** New orders appear on the screen with specific sandwich requirements.
2. **Ingredient Selection:** Players choose the correct ingredients from the inventory.
3. **Sandwich Assembly:** Players assemble the sandwich according to the order.
4. **Order Delivery:** The completed sandwich is delivered to the customer.
5. **Customer Feedback:** Customers react based on the sandwich's quality and delivery time.

Progression System:

- Players start with a basic sandwich shop and gradually unlock new ingredients, sandwich types, and equipment through gameplay and achievements.
- A leveling system could be implemented, with rewards for reaching new levels.

Challenge System:

- Increasingly demanding customers with more complex orders.
- Time-based challenges, such as rush hours or special events.
- Unexpected events, like equipment breakdowns or ingredient shortages.

Monetization:

- In-app purchases for additional ingredients, equipment, or decorations.
- Ad-supported free-to-play model with optional in-app purchases to remove ads.

Additional Features:

- **Customization:** Players can personalize their sandwich shop with decorations and themes.
- **Multiplayer:** Cooperative or competitive modes could be introduced, such as serving customers together or competing for the highest score.
- **Social Features:** Players can share their achievements, compete with friends, or participate in online challenges.

This core gameplay loop and system design provide a solid foundation for a fun and engaging sandwich shop simulator. By focusing on time management, customer satisfaction, and strategic decision-making, the game can offer a rewarding experience for players of all skill levels.

Would you like to explore specific game mechanics or system design elements in more detail?"

Again, this prompt and output was generated on the first try, in a few seconds, and is done virtually free – or at least for the end user generating these prompts. It also creates and adds on ideas generating that can very effectively support brainstorming game concept creation. This would have usually taken a few days of work for humans. AI can generate a near-free idea almost instantly. This reduces costs and speeds up ideation and creation when humans and AI work together.

Assuming similar inputs and outputs as our core concept example, the results of applying AI to mechanics and systems generation are the same. The cost efficiencies and productivity gains are identical. Similarly, the machine could also batch the previous step from a prompt engineer, which could, in turn, generate even more savings.

Gemini cost PAYG	Character length	Gemini Tokens	Cost per 1M token	Total cost
Input	135	34	$0.35	$0.0000119
Output	2801	701	$1.05	$0.00073605

Total				$0.000748

Mechanics & Systems	Human-only cost	AI-supplemented cost	Variation
Human cost	$2000	$100	-95%
AI/Tool cost	$0	$0.000748	
Total	**$2000**	**$100.000748**	**-95%**

M&S productivity	Human-only output	AI-supplemented output	Variation
M&S generation per cost efficiency calculation (40h)	1	20	+1900%
M&S generation in 1 week – unbatched 2m (40h)	1	1,200	+119,900%
M&S generation in 1 week - batched 2m (168h)	1	5,040	+503,900%
M&S generation in 1 week - batched 20s (168h)	1	30,240	+3,023,900%

6.1.3 Concept art creation

Core concept decisions are often supported with concept art. Usually, a Producer, Marketing, or ideation team will hire concept artists to create these images. Tools like DALL-E and Midjourney have made this task almost fully automated and instant. This step usually takes at least a week, often weeks. It involves a back-and-forth between the requestees and the artists. Now, it can be done directly by the requestee via an AI image generator.

> *"Je pense qu'au niveau de la créativité, de partir d'une page blanche, de générer une image de rien, là, ça peut servir à la pré-prod. Ça sert dans le greyboxing, au prototypage."*
>
> *AI translation: "I believe that, in terms of creativity, starting with a blank page and generating an image from scratch can be beneficial in pre-production. It's useful in greyboxing and prototyping."*
>
> —Interview with Pierre-Paul Giroux
> Vice-President Engineering A.I. at Unity

Regarding costs, DALL-E 3's pricing varies between $0.04 and $0.12 per image, and DALL-E 2's varies between $0.016 and $0.02 per image.[11] These are for "instant" requests. A user willing to batch his requests and able to wait up to 24 hours can lower these costs by an additional 50%.

Midjourney's pricing, assuming a medium to large corporation, would be $60 to $120 per month. This would provide unlimited usage for 15 to 25 concurrent users.

Classic concept artists charge between $200 and $1,000 per image. In contrast, this new AI is almost free.[12] Even assuming a basic project of 50 images at the low end of the human design cost spectrum and DALL-E's and Midjourney's costliest options, AI image generation would cost 98.8% to 99.99% less than traditional means.

Image output	Human design Low-end	Human design High-End	DALL-E 2 High cost	DALL-E 3 High cost	Midjourney High cost
1 image	$200	$1,000	$0.02	$0.12	$120
50 images	$10,000	$50,000	$1	$6	$120
250 images	$50,000	$250,000	$5	$30	$120
1000 images	$200,000	$1,000,000	$20	$120	$120

Image output	Human design Low-end	DALL-E 2 High cost	DALL-E 3 High cost	Midjourney High cost
50 images	$10,000	$1	$6	$120
Proportion - $10K	100.00%	0.01%	0.06%	1.20%
Variation	0.00%	-99.99%	-99.94%	-98.80%

Concept art	Human-only cost	AI-supplemented cost	Variation
Human cost	$10,000	$400	-96%
AI/Tool cost	$0	$120	
Total	**$10,000**	**$520**	**-94.8%**

Assuming DALL-E's costliest option, even after ten iterations of an image to get a desired result, AI costs would still be 166 to 833 times cheaper than sending this work to a concept artist. A cost reduction of 99.40% to 99.88% and achieved within a few seconds.

Even by overestimating a full day of work on this AI task to be conservative, the costliest platform would save almost 95% compared to traditional methods.

Using cost efficiency as a basis to calculate productivity would get an output of approximately 19 times more content. But the reality is that we can generate this content repeatedly, with many variations, or on entirely different themes. A more realistic scenario is that you could generate a new set every few minutes. Humans could supervise it or not; again, you could batch the work during the evenings and weekends. Work may need to be verified, but productivity would be up drastically. Nonetheless, it would likely be thousands of times more productive, considering a machine can generate a day's worth of work

[11] Pricing, OpenAI, https://openai.com/api/pricing/, 29 July 2024

[12] A guide to concept art estimation, M. Goodarzi, https://pixune.com/blog/concept-art-price/, 11 July 2024

in mere seconds. The calculations below illustrate this explanation, where a user can easily generate new images every 2 minutes, even with multiple iterations. A batched machine job could likely generate nearly 1,000 images per 8-hour day, 3,000 per 24 hours, and 20,000 per week per job. More if split properly by a prompt engineer.

Although these numbers are quite high, the more likely reality is the second option below, as a user would still need to verify the AI output and, in the best-case scenario, iterate on these outputs to produce better and better content, closer and closer to the desired and planned outcome. An end-user would likely not need 240 weeks' worth of concept art for a title, so there is a finite productivity plateau.

Concept art productivity	Human-only output	AI-supplemented output	Variation
Concept art generation per cost efficiency calculation (40h)	1	19.23	+1823%
Concept art generation in 1 day – unbatched 2m (8h)	0.2	240	+119,900%
Concept art generation in 1 day – batched 30s (8h)	0.2	960	+479,900%
Concept art generation in 1 day – batched 30s (24h)	0.2	2880	+1,439,900%
Concept art generation in 1 week – batched 30s (168h)	1	20,160	+2,015,900%

Artists and purists may balk at the concept of using a machine, advising that it's not art, that it's a copy, a fake, a machine's output. Aside from ethical or legal concerns, though, the quality output from these platforms matches some of the best artists out there. Tools like Leonardo.ai even allow training on proprietary datasets to generate these types of images.[13] Here are some quick examples using popular platforms to illustrate this point in various styles.

Prompt: "*Concept art for a Bladerunner type video game*"

Output:

[13] Training & Datasets, Leonardo.ai, https://app.leonardo.ai/training-datasets, July 2024

Midjourney 6.1 Picture 1

Midjourney 6.1 Picture 2

DALL-E 3 Picture 1

DALL-E 3 Picture 2

Midjourney6.1 Picture 3

Midjourney 6.1 Picture 4

DALL-E 3 Picture 3

DALL-E 3 Picture 4

Prompt: "*Hi *, can you please generate images of a 2d video game where a cat with a sword is fighting a dragon? 2d platformer style*"

Output:

Midjourney 6.1 Picture 1

Midjourney 6.1 Picture 2

DALL-E 3 Picture 1

DALL-E 3 Picture 2

Midjourney6.1 Picture 3

Midjourney 6.1 Picture 4

DALL-E 3 Picture 3

DALL-E 3 Picture 4

6.1.4 Storyboard, narrative & world design

Once concepts are greenlit for early production, an assigned team works on storyboards, narrative, and world design. This iterative process often changes throughout game development, but is mainly built in earlier stages of the process. Again, and as before, humans working alongside AI match standalone humans in quality, but they vastly outpace them in speed, productivity, and cost efficiency in content creation.

The following are example outputs from Gemini and Perplexity, each generated within a few seconds of the first prompt iteration. Note that we restructured the output from text-only solely for ease of reading and space optimization.

Prompt: "Hi *, can you generate a game storyboard based on a 2d video game where a cat with a sword is fighting a dragon please?"

Gemini Output: *(Restructured for ease of reading and space reduction)*

Cat vs. Dragon: A 2D Platformer Storyboard

Scene 1: Purrfect Peace

- Panel 1: Wide shot of a quaint village nestled amongst rolling green hills. A fluffy white cat (Mittens) sits contentedly on a windowsill, basking in the sun.
- Panel 2: Close-up on Mittens, eyes widening in shock as a monstrous shadow falls over the village.
- Panel 3: Establishing shot of a colossal black dragon soaring through the sky, smoke billowing from its nostrils.

Scene 2: Claws & Calls to Action

- Panel 1: Mittens leaps through the window, determined glint in its eyes.
- Panel 2: Inside the village elder's cottage, Mittens stands before a wizened old cat pointing a paw towards a dusty suit of armor.
- Panel 3: Close-up on the armor - a miniature suit of gleaming silver with a tiny sword and shield.

Scene 3: Suit Up & Sword Up

- Panel 1: Montage sequence showing Mittens struggling to put on the armor, looking increasingly comical.
- Panel 2: Mittens, finally suited up, looking fierce (as fierce as a fluffy cat can) holding the miniature sword aloft.
- Panel 3: The elder cat pats Mittens on the head, a determined nod exchanged between them.

Scene 4: The Climb

- Panel 1: Wide shot of the imposing dragon perched atop a dormant volcano. Lava flows ominously down the slopes.
- Panel 2: Mittens stands at the foot of the volcano, looking up with a determined expression.
- Panel 3: Montage sequence showing Mittens climbing the treacherous slopes, dodging falling rocks and leaping over fiery chasms.

Scene 5: The Showdown

- Panel 1: Wide shot of the volcano peak. The dragon rears back, preparing to unleash a fiery breath attack.
- Panel 2: Mittens stands bravely before the dragon, sword held high.
- Panel 3: Close-up on Mittens, eyes narrowed in concentration as it leaps towards the dragon, dodging the fiery breath.

Scene 6: Claws vs. Claws

- Panel 1: Action shot of Mittens using its agility to dodge the dragon's swipes and bites.
- Panel 2: Close-up on Mittens landing a critical blow with its sword on the dragon's paw.
- Panel 3: The dragon roars in pain, momentarily stunned.

Scene 7: Feline Fury

- Panel 1: Wide shot of the volcano peak. The dragon looks enraged, smoke billowing from its nostrils.
- Panel 2: Mittens charges forward with a battle cry.
- Panel 3: Close-up on Mittens delivering a final blow to the dragon's snout, sending it reeling back.

Scene 8: Victory Lap

- Panel 1: The dragon crashes defeated onto the slopes of the volcano.
- Panel 2: Mittens stands triumphantly atop the peak, the village cheering in the distance.
- Panel 3: Close-up on Mittens, shedding its armor and reverting to its fluffy self, a proud smile on its face.

Perplexity output: *(Restructured for ease of reading and space reduction)*

Game Title: "Whiskers & Steel: The Dragon's Bane"

Opening Scene

- A peaceful village of anthropomorphic cats
- Sudden attack by a massive dragon, breathing fire and destroying buildings
- Our hero, a brave cat named Whiskers, grabs his father's enchanted sword

Level 1: Village Escape

- Whiskers navigates burning village, dodging falling debris
- Tutorial on basic movement and sword swinging
- Encounters minor dragon minions (lizards, bats)
- Reaches village outskirts, sees dragon flying towards mountain lair

Level 2: Forest Adventure

- Whiskers enters dense forest
- Learns advanced combat moves against forest creatures
- Discovers hidden cave with power-up (magical armor)
- Exits forest, sees distant mountain with dragon circling peak

Level 3: Mountain Ascent

- Treacherous climb up rocky mountain paths
- Battles against dragon's minions become more intense
- Mid-level boss fight against dragon's lieutenant (a large griffin)
- Reaches dragon's lair entrance

Level 4: Dragon's Lair

- Navigates through trap-filled cave system
- Solves puzzles to unlock path to inner sanctum
- Finds legendary cat artifact that enhances sword's power
- Confronts dragon in its treasure room

Final Boss Battle

- Epic fight against the dragon, utilizing all learned skills
- Dragon uses various attacks: fire breath, tail swipes, flying charges
- Whiskers must target weak spots and dodge attacks
- After intense battle, Whiskers delivers final blow

Ending Scene

- Dragon defeated, lair begins to collapse
- Whiskers escapes with some treasure
- Returns to village as hero, celebration ensues
- Teaser for potential sequel (dragon egg hidden in rubble)

Again, creating such a board would have taken at least 1 or 2 people for a week to generate, often more. Should the reader decide that quality isn't up to par, note that this is only the first prompt iteration's output and can be reiterated with variations semi-indefinitely. Also, these were generated in a few seconds. So, they can be used in the creative process and the back-and-forth decision-making among game stakeholders. Without AI, this process can be quite time-consuming, costly, and often underestimated in impact.

Additionally, as mentioned earlier, stories and content undergo changes and evolution during game production for various reasons, including budget constraints, feasibility, narrative development, and market feedback. A fast, agile tool is often preferable to a slow, costly one, especially when the quality difference between the two options is minimal.

Regarding cost performance, comparatives are very similar to core concept development costs or those of game mechanics and system design, considering that we've used the same or similar LLM solution in these examples. The cost would have been less than 1/10th of a cent using Gemini.

Gemini storyboard	Human-only cost	AI-supplemented cost	Variation
Human cost	$2000	$100	-95%
AI/Tool cost	$0	$0.0007	
Total	**$2000**	**$100.0007**	**-95%**

Perplexity has a different pricing model for unlimited use under a subscription.[14] Compared to staff costs using traditional creation methods, it is low-cost, starting at $40/month or $400/year per seat for enterprise pricing. Assuming ≈1/4 of that monthly cost is used to consider proportionate usage, cost variation is only affected by 0.5%.

This 1/4 would still be a conservative and likely costlier way of calculating the price burden. It assumes that the assigned platform user will use its tools solely for the purpose of this project for a week, despite our estimated that this work will take only a couple of hours. A more optimistic, yet accurate, way of calculating these costs would yield comparable values to Gemini.

Perplexity storyboard	Human-only cost	AI-supplemented cost	Variation
Human cost	$2000	$100	-95%
AI/Tool cost	$0	$10	
Total	**$2000**	**$110**	**-94.5%**

> *"I think that a new skill set will have to emerge, identifying when is the right time to use Gen AI, and when it should be avoided."*
>
> —Interview with Jamie Campbell
> Founder of MTX Solutions, Co-Founder of d3t Studio, ex-ATI (AMD), ex-Technical Director at THQ

Again, productivity gains are very similar to core concept development costs or those of game mechanics and system design. We've used the same or a similar LLM solution in these examples.

Storyboard productivity	Human-only output	AI-supplemented output	Variation
Storyboard generation per cost efficiency calculation (40h)	1	20	+1900%
Storyboard generation in 1 week – unbatched 2m (40h)	1	1200	+119 900%

[14] Perplexity – Enterprise Pro, Perplexity, https://www.perplexity.ai/enterprise, August 2024

Storyboard generation in 1 week - batched 2m (168h)	1	5040	+503 900%
Storyboard generation in 1 week - batched 20s (168h)	1	30 240	+3 023 900%

"L'IA peut devenir un partenaire de création, si on prend le temps de la nourrir de notre vision. Je lui donne du contexte, je l'implique dans ma réflexion, et elle me propose des variantes en phase avec ma sensibilité. Je peux ainsi dessiner une scène, discuter avec elle de ce que je ressens, ajuster, recommencer... et en quelques heures, co-créer l'animation de trois personnages distincts. Ce n'est pas qu'un gain de temps — c'est un dialogue accéléré entre deux imaginaires."

AI translation: "AI can become a creative partner if we take the time to share our vision with it. I give it context, involve it in my thinking, and it offers me variations in line with my sensibilities. I can thus sketch a scene, discuss with it what I feel, adjust, start over... and in a few hours, co-create the animation of three distinct characters. It's not just a time saver—it's an accelerated dialogue between two minds."

—Interview with Frederic Vicaire
Founder and Creative Director of art!equin agency

6.1.5 Scriptwriting

Scriptwriting follows suit to this creative process. For the sake of not repeating myself, though, this process can also be supported or replaced by LLM platforms and has, as such, very similar AI cost efficiency and productivity gains as the previous examples using those types of solutions. Below are the follow-up LLM examples using Gemini and Perplexity.

Prompt (following storyboard request): "Thanks, can you write me a script for that first scene please?"

Gemini Output:

Scene 1: Purrfect Peace
[FADE IN]
EXT. VILLAGE - DAY
A quaint village nestled amongst rolling green hills basks in the warm afternoon sun. Smoke curls lazily from chimneys, and children play in a central square.

CLOSE UP - MITTENS (WHITE CAT)
Mittens, a fluffy white cat with bright green eyes, sits contentedly on a windowsill, enjoying the gentle breeze. It lazily grooms its fur and purrs softly.
Suddenly, a GIANT SHADOW falls across the village, plunging everything into a brief moment of darkness.
MITTENS (CONT'D)
Eyes widening in shock, Mittens whips its head around, looking towards the source of the shadow.
PAN UP
A colossal BLACK DRAGON with fiery red eyes and massive leathery wings soars through the sky. Smoke billows from its nostrils, obscuring the sun.
SOUND: A low, menacing growl emanates from the dragon.
WIDE SHOT - VILLAGE
Villagers scream and run for cover as the dragon lets out a fiery BREATH, engulfing the outskirts of the village in flames.
MITTENS (CONT'D)
Eyes filled with newfound determination, Mittens leaps through the broken window, landing gracefully on the cobblestone street below.
[FADE OUT]

Perplexity output:

Certainly! Here's a script for the opening scene of "Whiskers & Steel: The Dragon's Bane":

Opening Scene: The Dragon's Attack

[FADE IN: A peaceful cat village at dawn. Anthropomorphic cats are going about their daily routines.]

NARRATOR (V.O.): In the land of Felinia, where cats walk on two legs and live in harmony, a new day dawns in the village of Whiskerton.

[Camera pans across the village, showing cats opening shops, children playing, and farmers tending crops.]

WHISKERS (young cat, our hero): Dad, can I practice with your sword today?

FATHER: Not today, son. Remember, a true warrior—

[Suddenly, a dark shadow passes overhead. Cats look up, confused.]

VILLAGE ELDER: By my whiskers! What is that?

[A massive dragon swoops down, breathing fire. Buildings catch aflame, cats scatter in panic.]

DRAGON: Raaaawwrr! Your village is mine, little cats!

MOTHER: Whiskers! Get inside, quickly!

[Whiskers runs towards home but stops, seeing his father grab his sword.]

FATHER: I must defend our village! Whiskers, stay with your mother!

[The dragon lands, crushing a building. Cats flee in all directions.]

WHISKERS: Dad, no!

[Whiskers' father charges at the dragon but is swatted aside. His enchanted sword clatters to the ground near Whiskers.]

DRAGON: Is this the best Whiskerton can offer? Pathetic!

[Whiskers looks at the sword, then at the dragon destroying his village. Determination fills his eyes.]

WHISKERS: (whispers) I'm sorry, Mom.

[He grabs the sword, which glows faintly in his paws.]

WHISKERS: (shouting) Hey, you overgrown lizard!

[The dragon turns, eyeing Whiskers with amusement.]
DRAGON: Oh? And what do we have here? A kitten with a toothpick?
WHISKERS: (voice shaking but determined) I... I challenge you! Leave our village alone!
DRAGON: (laughing) Very well, little one. Show me what you've got!
[Whiskers grips the sword tightly, standing his ground as the dragon looms over him.]
NARRATOR (V.O.): And so began the legend of Whiskers, the unlikeliest of heroes in the land of Felinia.
[FADE TO BLACK]
[Text appears: "Whiskers & Steel: The Dragon's Bane"]
[FADE OUT]

> *"As people improve at prompting, the equation starts to change. When you can get a good result on the first or second try instead of the twentieth, it becomes faster than doing the work manually. If you know how to shape the prompt, the tool becomes truly efficient."*
>
> —Interview with Stephen Peacock
> Director AI at 2K, Ex-Head of AI at AWS & Keywords

In addition to broad-access LLMs for the sake of scriptwriting, large publishers are developing their own AI tools that are custom-built for their needs. An example is Ubisoft's proprietary Ghostwriter tool, which enables automated writing of NPC chatter. [15]

Although script writing is text-heavy compared to core concept creation or storyboarding, its impact on overall cost is also limited, considering LLM costs are relatively low. Assuming the same cost structure, even with a heavier output load of 75,000 characters (approximately 15,000 words), we develop an AI cost of less than 2 cents through Gemini's pay-as-you-go model.

Gemini cost PAYG	Character length	Gemini Tokens	Cost per 1M token	Total cost
Input	200	50	$0.35	$0.0000175
Output	75,000	18,750	$1.05	$0.0196875
Total				**$0.0197050**

An average script writer would take 2-3 weeks to write a script of that length. We'll assume 2 weeks to be conservative and in favor of humans. We'll also assume that it'll take more than one attempt from

[15] The Convergence of AI and Creativity: Introducing Ghostwriter, R. Barth, Ubisoft, https://news.ubisoft.com/en-us/article/7Cm07zbBGy4Xml6WgYi25d/the-convergence-of-ai-and-creativity-introducing-ghostwriter, 21 March 2023

humans to reiterate, rewrite, and review the text from the AI platform. I've estimated 8 hours instead of the 2 hours used in previous similar examples.

Gemini script writing	Human-only cost	AI-supplemented cost	Variation
Human cost	$2000	$400	-80%
AI/Tool cost	$0	$0.02	
Total	**$2000**	**$400.02**	**-80%**

Again, we can use the same concepts of cost efficiency to calculate productivity here as in other examples, as we use the same type of LLM-supported solution. We could extrapolate even further as we did for the other examples. Still, considering the high amount of content that would need to be verified, reviewed, and edited by the human eye, the gains may be pretty limited. There's so much content a human can read and review per day. The above assumes 15,000 words per day; thus, the following is an entire week's worth of 75,000 words.

Script writing productivity	Human-only output	AI-supplemented output	Variation
Script writing generation per cost efficiency calculation (40h)	1	5	+400%

6.1.6 Documentation and communication

One of the cornerstones of game design is the Game Design Document (GDD). It's a comprehensive document that outlines each aspect of the game. It serves as the primary blueprint for the team and is an essential communication tool for all stakeholders. It's a roadmap that guides the entire game development team. It ensures a shared vision between team members, provides an organizational framework, and serves as a reference.

Considering the output is mainly text, LLM platforms can effectively support the creative writing necessary to build the document, as well as management and planning tasks. Below is another example using Perplexity.

Prompt: "Hi P, per the previous requests in this thread, can you please write me a Game Design Document (GDD) for the game 'Whiskers & Steel: The Dragon's Bane'?"

Perplexity output:

Game Design Document (GDD) for "Whiskers & Steel: The Dragon's Bane"

1. **Game Overview**

- **Game Title**: Whiskers & Steel: The Dragon's Bane
- **Genre**: 2D Action-Adventure Platformer
- **Target Audience**: Ages 10 and up, fans of action-adventure and platformer games
- **Platform**: PC, Console (Nintendo Switch, PlayStation, Xbox)
- **Game Concept**: "Whiskers & Steel: The Dragon's Bane" is a 2D action-adventure platformer where players control Whiskers, a brave cat armed with an enchanted sword, on a quest to save his

village from a menacing dragon. The game combines fast-paced combat, platforming challenges, and puzzle-solving elements across various environments.

2. **Story and Characters**

Story Summary: In the peaceful village of Whiskerton, anthropomorphic cats live in harmony until a dragon attacks, burning the village and causing chaos. Whiskers, a young cat, takes up his father's enchanted sword to fight the dragon and save his home. His journey takes him through forests, mountains, and the dragon's lair, where he faces numerous enemies and challenges.

Main Characters:

- **Whiskers**: The protagonist, a brave young cat with a strong sense of justice. Equipped with his father's enchanted sword.
- **Dragon**: The primary antagonist, a fearsome creature threatening the village.
- **Father**: Whiskers' father, a former warrior who is injured during the dragon's attack.
- **Village Elder**: Provides guidance and wisdom to Whiskers.
- **Mother**: Whiskers' caring and protective mother.

3. **Gameplay Mechanics**

Core Gameplay:

- **Combat**: Sword attacks, combos, and special moves. Players can upgrade Whiskers' abilities and sword.
- **Platforming**: Jumping, climbing, and dodging obstacles.
- **Puzzle-Solving**: Environmental puzzles that require players to use their wits and Whiskers' abilities.
- **Exploration**: Discover hidden areas, collect power-ups, and gather resources.

Controls:

- **Movement**: Arrow keys or joystick
- **Jump**: Spacebar or A button
- **Attack**: Left mouse button or X button
- **Special Move**: Right mouse button or Y button
- **Interact**: E key or B button

4. **Game Progression**

Levels:

1. **Village Escape**: Tutorial level where Whiskers learns basic controls and escapes the burning village.
2. **Forest Adventure**: Introduces advanced combat and environmental puzzles.
3. **Mountain Ascent**: Features challenging platforming and a mid-level boss fight.
4. **Dragon's Lair**: Final level with complex puzzles and the ultimate boss battle against the dragon.

Objectives:

- **Primary**: Defeat the dragon and save the village.
- **Secondary**: Collect hidden artifacts, rescue villagers, and upgrade Whiskers' abilities.

5. **World and Level Design**

Art Style:

- **Visuals**: Hand-drawn 2D art with vibrant colors and detailed environments.
- **Characters**: Anthropomorphic cats with expressive animations.
- **Enemies**: Varied designs including lizards, bats, and mythical creatures.

Level Themes:

- **Village**: Burning buildings, panicked NPCs, and falling debris.
- **Forest**: Dense trees, hidden caves, and magical creatures.
- **Mountain**: Rocky paths, steep cliffs, and treacherous terrain.
- **Lair**: Dark caves, traps, and treasure rooms.

6. **Assets**

Visual Assets:

- **Character Sprites**: Whiskers, dragon, NPCs, enemies.
- **Backgrounds**: Village, forest, mountain, lair.
- **Objects**: Sword, power-ups, environmental elements.

Audio Assets:

- **Music**: Dynamic soundtrack that changes with the environment.
- **Sound Effects**: Sword swings, enemy attacks, environmental sounds.
- **Voice Acting**: Narration, character dialogues.

7. **Technical Specifications**

- **Engine**: Unity
- **Resolution**: 1920x1080 (HD)
- **Frame Rate**: 60 FPS
- **Platforms**: PC, Nintendo Switch, PlayStation, Xbox

8. **Milestones and Timeline**

Pre-Production:

- Concept Art and Storyboarding: 2 months
- Prototype Development: 3 months

Production:

- Level Design and Asset Creation: 6 months
- Programming and Mechanics Implementation: 6 months
- Alpha Testing: 2 months

Post-Production:

- Beta Testing and Bug Fixing: 3 months
- Marketing and Release Preparation: 2 months
- Launch: 1 month

9. **Team and Roles**

- **Project Lead**: Oversees the project and ensures milestones are met.
- **Game Designer**: Develops gameplay mechanics and level design.
- **Programmers**: Implement game mechanics and systems.
- **Artists**: Create character designs, backgrounds, and animations.
- **Sound Designers**: Compose music and create sound effects.
- **QA Testers**: Test the game for bugs and provide feedback.

This Game Design Document outlines the essential elements of "Whiskers & Steel: The Dragon's Bane," providing a clear roadmap for development and ensuring all team members are aligned with the project's vision.

A true GDD is longer than this, but LLMs enable us to expand quickly on one section or another, generating the complete documentation needed or at least supplying most of what is required.

A GDD's complexity and size are similar to those of a script, so the latter example is a better reference for the amount of time and effort needed to generate it (8 hours, while AI-supported). Although this document typically evolves and changes with the team, we will use the original creation as the basis for performance calculations. We can assume that future edits could also be AI-supported.

Gemini GDD creation	Human-only cost	AI-supplemented cost	Variation
Human cost	$2000	$400	-80%
AI/Tool cost	$0	$0.01	
Total	**$2000**	**$400.01**	**-80%**

Again, productivity gains are very similar to core concept development costs or those of game mechanics and system design, considering that we've used the same or similar LLM solution in these examples.

GDD creation productivity	Human-only output	AI-supplemented output	Variation
GDD creation generation per cost efficiency calculation (40h)	1	5	+400%

"Rather than using natural language to describe a game, and have a large language model pipe a game out of the other end, I think it's going to be incremental improvements that will have the biggest impact. Just because the of scale, if you've got hundreds, thousands, of engineers, if you can get a small percentage gain in their productivity, it adds up to quite a lot."

—Interview with Jamie Campbell
Founder of MTX Solutions, Co-Founder of d3t Studio, ex-ATI (AMD), ex-Technical Director at THQ

6.2 Game Engineering

Game engineering and coding are the core, and arguably the main aspects, of game development. The process focuses on the technical implementation of the game design discussed in the previous section. It involves the application of computer science, mathematics, and software engineering to create the base code that brings the game to life. The required coding involves translating game design concepts into programming languages. This code creates the game's logic, physics, and interactions and integrates the visual and audio assets within the game.

> *"Le gain en efficacité (AI) dépend vraiment du contexte. Dans certains cas c'est 99%. Dans d'autres cas ce n'est pas applicable et c'est 0%."*
>
> *AI translation: "The AI efficiency gain really depends on the context. In some cases, it's 99%. In others, it's not applicable and it's 0%."*
>
> —Interview with Stéphanie Bouchard
> Freelance Game Designer/Director - Oxitocyn
> Ex Leadership & AI positions at Stockholm Syndrome.AI, Red Barrels, WBGM, Ubisoft, THQ
> Ex Game Teacher at NAD-UQAC, Campus ADN, Champlain College, Dawson College
> Research contributor at MIT and Concordia University

The following analysis demonstrates a 10% cost efficiency gain by using AI-assisted platforms to support game developers' code generation. Some researchers are finding cost efficiency gains of up to 30% and even 55%, but these are for less complex tasks that are irrelevant in this context.

> *"If we're talking about blank piece of paper, start writing some code, I think we could probably see reasonable improvements there, Maybe 10%, 15%, 20% improvement."*
>
> *"If we're making the assumption of getting to the same result, I think that you could get up to 20% cost savings. What would naturally happen if we got those productivity gains, though, is that saved time would be reinvested into the work. It would then expand to fill that vacuum. So the gain is likely less."*
>
> —Interview with Jamie Campbell
> Founder of MTX Solutions, Co-Founder of d3t Studio, ex-ATI (AMD), ex-Technical Director at THQ

Game Engineering costs	Human-only cost	AI-supplemented cost		Variation
		Human	AI[16]	
Game Engineering	$94,000	$84,600	$100	-9.9%
Total	**$94,000**	**$84,700**		**-9.9%**

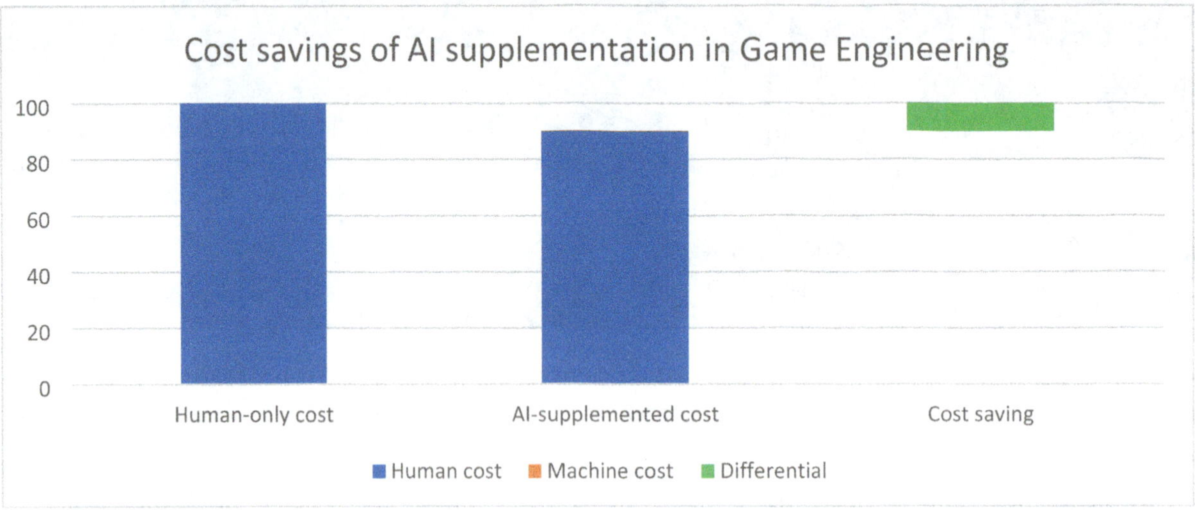

[16] About billing for GitHub Copilot Individual, GitHub Docs, https://docs.github.com/en/copilot/managing-copilot/managing-copilot-as-an-individual-subscriber/managing-your-copilot-subscription/about-billing-for-github-copilot-individual, October 2024

> *"I think there's, an exponential curve, which is how homogenized, how defined, and how strict the code is that the AI is being asked to work on. Because the more that you can constrict that envelope, the better a Gen AI solution is going to work with it.*
> *If you've got an engine that you've written yourself, and it's got no coding conventions, and it's got bits and pieces of stuff hanging all over the place, how can you expect a machine to deal with that efficiently? If you've got something that's got rigorous coding standards, that you can train, you can drop a reference document into an LLM and tell it, this is our coding convention, you'll get way better results."*
>
> —Interview with Jamie Campbell
> Founder of MTX Solutions, Co-Founder of d3t Studio, ex-ATI (AMD), ex-Technical Director at THQ

Extracting productivity gains from these calculations would reveal a similarly modest productivity output gain of 11% from leveraging AI coding support in games compared to human-only approaches.

Game Engineering output	Human-only output	AI-supplemented output
Output	1	1.1098
Productivity gains		**10.98%**

Game Engineering output	Human-only Human cost & output	AI-supplemented Human cost & output	AI-supplemented Machine cost	AI-supplemented Machine output
Value 1	$94,000	$84,600	$100	$9,400
Ratio 1	100.00%	90.00%	0.11%	10.00%
Ratio AI-sup	110.98%	**99.88%**	0.12%	**11.10%**

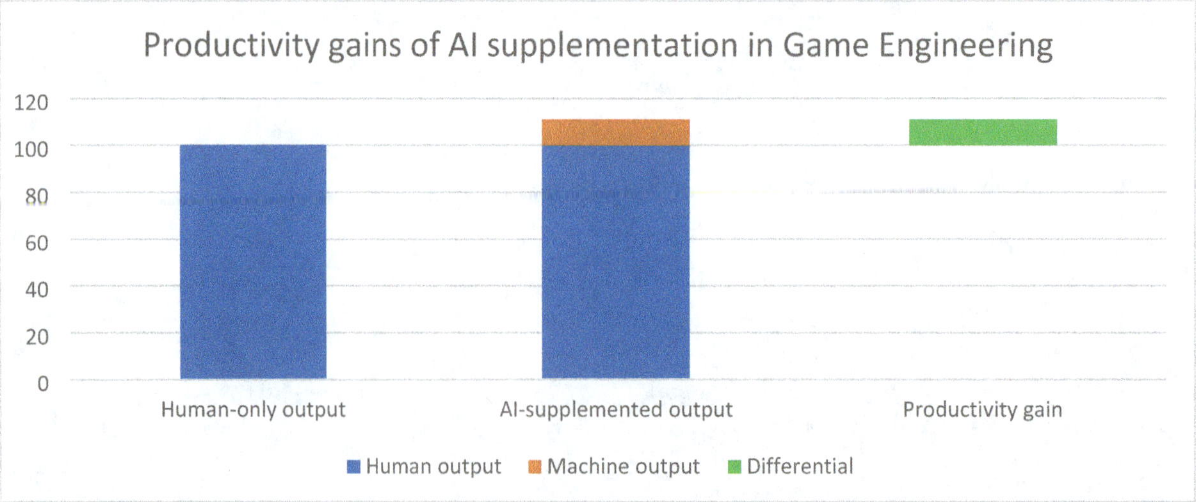

Note that, as addressed in the following section, these numbers could be conservative and that, because of rapidly evolving AI tools, they could quickly improve.

> *"AI needs to be used effectively. Certain practices can lead to wasting a lot of people's time. You'll be able to generate a lot of content, but it doesn't mean it's useful. It may just help everybody waste more time more effectively."*
>
> -Interview with Matt Ditton
> CEO and Co-Founder of Mighty Games Group & Mighty Build and Test

Delving into the data, multiple experiments with AI-supported game coding have revealed several constants.[17,18,19,20]

1. Output quality changes drastically depending on the source data. If the training data fed to the AI is good, there's a higher chance of a higher-quality output.
2. Code complexity has an essential impact on output quality. A simple application is relatively easy to generate for an AI. However, complex systems or algorithms, especially those with interdependence between systems, can be more prone to errors, even more so if the intent isn't understood.

---

[17] How good is enough? AI vs. human code, SAP LeanIX, https://engineering.leanix.net/blog/ai-vs-human-code/, 16 Dec 2022

[18] Project AVA: Game development with AI, Keywords Studios, GDC 2004, https://www.keywordsstudios.com/en/ava-at-gdc/, April 2024

[19] Productivity Assessment of Neural Code Completion, GitHub team, https://dl.acm.org/doi/pdf/10.1145/3520312.3534864, 12 June 2022

[20] Scientifically Measuring the True Impact of Generative AI Software Development, A. Girzhadovich, Exadel, https://exadel.com/news/measuring-generative-ai-software-development/, 14 May 2024

a. OpenAI themselves advise that ChatGPT can "occasionally produce incorrect answers" and may produce "harmful instructions or biased content". [21] Unfortunately, in the case of coding, sometimes the only thing needed for a whole program not to run properly is an "occasionally produced incorrect answer".
b. Games are complex and interdependent by nature. Newer games being released are also getting larger and more complex. Thus, AI-generated content, in this context, can be highly prone to errors.
c. "Easy" tasks are where AI generation can be efficient. Some of the more successful game code tasks often cited are porting or remastering between platforms and/or code languages. These have a predefined intent and outcome, and the differences between the source and target code are minimal and easily identifiable.

3. Although AI generates code much faster than humans, the output quality is not entirely satisfactory yet. As such, for complex tasks, the time saved during AI code generation is often more than negated by the time a human would need to understand the AI code, correct and remove the errors injected into it.
4. The expertise of the user using the AI platform significantly impacts efficiency. There's no "intent" behind the AI-generated code, and as such, the actual code outcome can often be quite different from what was originally intended by the prompter. Experienced expert prompters can input more effective requests and thus achieve better output.
5. The expertise of the user writing the code has a significant impact on efficiency. Very senior coders, who can easily read, see, and understand what the machine is trying to do, can rapidly find and correct the errors injected in the code by AI. An inexperienced coder won't understand or find the code issues generated by AI and can sometimes waste more time correcting issues than if they had generated the code themselves.
6. The output quality and the number of AI tools available for these tasks are increasing rapidly.
7. The cost of these tools and platforms is low, especially compared to the hourly wages saved and/or output increased by their use.
8. Developers don't spend 100% of their days writing code. Coding is usually a fraction of what coders do. On average, developers spend more time discovering, researching, and experimenting than coding. As such, even 100% code-writing automation would only automate a fraction of their days, tasks, efforts, and costs.

[21] What is ChatGPT?, OpenAI, https://help.openai.com/en/articles/6783457-what-is-chatgpt, August 2024

"Le gain en efficacité dépend de la complexité du jeu. Street Fighter est plus facile à résoudre que Watch Dogs. Les NPC ont plus d'affaires à faire dans plus de sphères différentes. Plus tu as de sphères, plus c'est dur à entraîner."

AI translation: "The efficiency gain depends on the game's complexity. Street Fighter is easier to solve than Watch Dogs. NPCs have more stuff to do in more different spheres. The more spheres you have, the harder it is to train."

—Interview with Stéphanie Bouchard
Freelance Game Designer/Director - Oxitocyn
Ex Leadership & AI positions at Stockholm Syndrome.AI, Red Barrels, WBGM, Ubisoft, THQ
Ex Game Teacher at NAD-UQAC, Campus ADN, Champlain College, Dawson College
Research contributor at MIT and Concordia University

"VS (Visual Studio) Code is the most popular code editor. Cursor is a fork of it, and it's very AI integrated. It allows you to have AI, like ChatGPT, see your entire code base, and you can ask it questions. I don't just generate code and be done with it. I can highlight a big block of code and ask the AI questions about it. Like: How can I refactor this to be more elegant? What are alternative solutions? Things like this is by far my biggest use."

—Interview with Dylan Ebert, PhD
Developer Advocate Engineer, Hugging Face

A research team at the US Department of Energy's Oak Ridge Lab speculates that by 2040, LLMs will write better and faster code than the best human developers.[22] Currently, the efficiency output from these tools and platforms varies significantly. Current user—and organization-reported efficiency gains range from nearly 0% to over 50%.

[22] Will humans even write code in 2040 and what would that mean for extreme heterogeneity in computing?, Oak Ridge National Laboratory, https://arxiv.org/pdf/1712.00676, 19 Dec 2017

"We're able to have the same output, but cheaper. [...]
It's just a tooling situation. There used to be teams of Engine people, but now you can simply buy Unreal or Unity. Job done. It's the same with AI tools."

—Interview with Matt Ditton
CEO and Co-Founder of Mighty Games Group & Mighty Build and Test

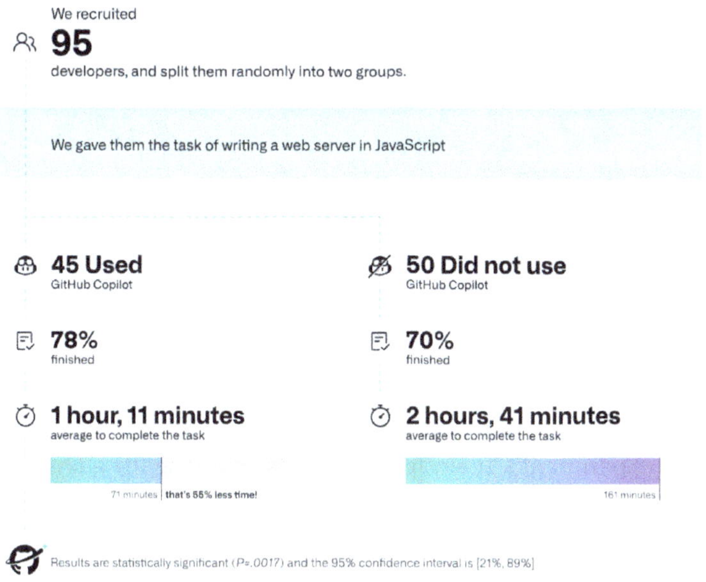

First, looking at more positive results, GitHub reports that in one experiment deployed through 95 developers, using Copilot, their AI programming support tool, allowed for an average efficiency gain of 55%.[23]

It is worth noting that the task was relatively simple compared to a more complex game: writing a web server in JavaScript. It's also a task where the AI tool has broad access to repeated relevant data sources to recreate. Additionally, while GitHub is widely used in software development, it is less prevalent in gaming, where other comparable tools, such as Perforce, are more commonly used. Both tools can be connected, though.

"Use Three.js as an example. I could paste code from Three.js, ask GenAI to analyze the structure, ask how I could translate this to what my goals are. This way of working, in that situation, it's probably about 10x productivity. Because it's learning and doing at the same time."

—Interview with Dylan Ebert, PhD
Developer Advocate Engineer, Hugging Face

---

[23]Research: quantifying GitHub Copilot's impact on developer productivity and happiness, GitHub, https://github.blog/news-insights/research/research-quantifying-github-copilots-impact-on-developer-productivity-and-happiness/, 21 May 2024

“Un jeu comme Watch Dogs prend au moins 3 personnes; 1 game designer senior et 2 programmeurs, pendant 2 à 3 ans. [...] Si tu entraînes un NPC pour Call of Duty avec du data de joueur, tu peux réentraîner un roaster au complet en 24 heures. [...] L'économie est de presque 100%.”

AI translation: "A game like Watch Dogs takes at least 3 people; 1 senior game designer and 2 programmers, for 2 to 3 years. [...] If you train an NPC for Call of Duty with player data, you can re-train an entire roaster in 24 hours. [...] The savings are almost 100%."

—Interview with Stéphanie Bouchard
Freelance Game Designer/Director - Oxitocyn
Ex Leadership & AI positions at Stockholm Syndrome.AI, Red Barrels, WBGM, Ubisoft, THQ
Ex Game Teacher at NAD-UQAC, Campus ADN, Champlain College, Dawson College
Research contributor at MIT and Concordia University

An external team at Faros.ai recreated a similar experiment with Copilot, collaborating with their own teams on a range of tasks over the course of a year. They achieved similar results, with a 55% reduction in lead time to production.[24] A survey of the experiment's team found that their efficiency gains were mostly due to avoiding the dreaded blank page syndrome. They report that it’s often easier to edit an AI-driven suggestion than start coding from nothing.

[24] Is GitHub Copilot Worth It? Real-World Data Reveals the Answer, Faros.ai, https://www.faros.ai/blog/is-github-copilot-worth-it-real-world-data-reveals-the-answer, 17 May 2024

"Using AI makes me 4 times faster than before, and a lot of it is the speed in which I learn. If you think about stack overflow, it's the old way to solve a problem; you look up for solutions on it. I see AI as a stack overflow that has access to all GitHub repositories. There's a lot of information. When I was making a city builder for the first time, there was no Chat GPT, and a city builder has a lot of specialized advanced knowledge that is not easy to find. But now, AI has access to all these repositories and knows about city builder architecture. Suddenly, I have access to a ton of information I could not have gotten without having worked in a city builder company. It made me learn way faster."

—Interview with Dylan Ebert, PhD
Developer Advocate Engineer, Hugging Face

On a more suggestive basis, the engineers surveyed by GitHub raised points related to self-satisfaction and well-being, which also improved the productivity of the end users. Developers felt more fulfilled and less frustrated. They could skip tedious tasks and focus on fun ones. They got into "the flow" more quickly and for more extended periods.

"The framework's already built for you, and you follow those coding conventions. So it's much easier for the co-pilots to present code in a way that you can plug it in and go. So I think that that will be a big productivity gain for people."

—Interview with Jamie Campbell
Founder of MTX Solutions, Co-Founder of d3t Studio, ex-ATI (AMD), ex-Technical Director at THQ

One caveat, though. Although Copilot appears to accelerate code development, some studies suggest that it, along with other AI code support tools, may actually slow down code maintenance —a key indicator of code quality. A study by GitClear, a software engineering platform, predicts that code churn on GitHub will double in 2024 compared to 2021, before the availability of AI support.[25] Code churn is the percentage of code reverted or updated within two weeks of its creation. In this case, the reason is assumed to be a reduced quality of output ever since AI coding support is available.

---

[25] Coding on Copilot, GitClear, https://gitclear-public.s3.us-west-2.amazonaws.com/Coding-on-Copilot-2024-Developer-Research.pdf, 16 Jan 2024

"There's a sweet spot in the middle of the skill curve where these tools are most useful. If you're brand new, tools like GitHub Copilot often suggest poor solutions, and you may not have the experience to recognize them. For mid-level developers, the value is much higher. You know enough to course-correct when things go wrong, but you still benefit from not having to recall every syntax or library. At the expert level, the benefit fades again. The tool doesn't know anything you don't already know."

—Interview with Stephen Peacock
Director AI at 2K, Ex-Head of AI at AWS & Keywords

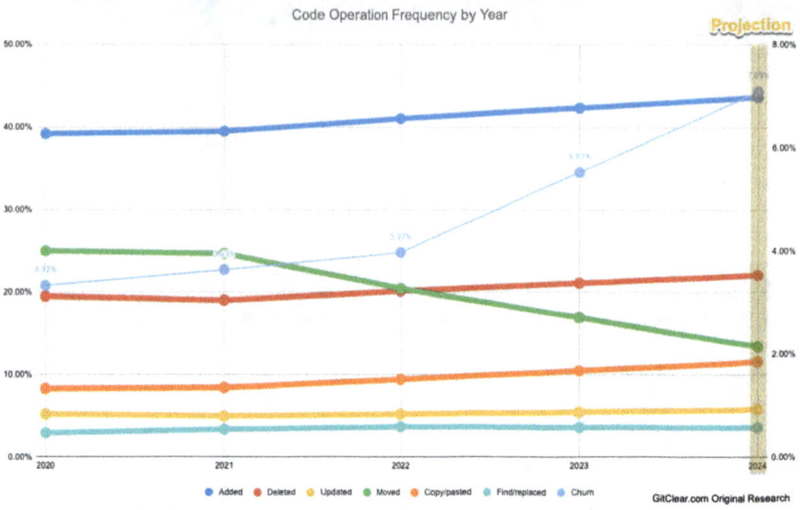

The research also raises a significant conundrum. Less experienced developers tend to use AI support more than experienced ones. However, experienced ones have a better and more informed understanding of what good code is and how costly lousy code is to maintain in the long run. AI code support is improving, but it can still be challenging to identify issues it introduces.

> *"One of the areas of concern, is LLMs like Claude are good at generating code. They do a good job of it and they write sophisticated code that does its job and it is fairly optimal. The biggest problem with it comes when it generates buggy code that appears to work but goes haywire in certain circumstances. Now for an experienced coder that's fine. They're used to dealing with that. They can unwind the code. They can even disassemble it if they want and go right down to machine code level and figure out what's going wrong. But for less experienced programmers, that's a big problem because the code looks right, but it's not working right, and you end up with that kind of false confidence and assuming that what the LLM has written is good when it's actually not. And it could actually be more time-consuming to figure out what's going wrong with that piece of code that looks right than it would have been to write the code in the first place."*
>
> —Interview with Jamie Campbell
> Founder of MTX Solutions, Co-Founder of d3t Studio, ex-ATI (AMD), ex-Technical Director at THQ

Exadel did a different experiment, including using not only GitHub Copilot but also ChatGPT-4 Turbo. They also provided those tools to non-coding specialists, such as product owners and Scrum Masters. They argued that the latter's efficiency also affects product creation and delivery. The experiment lasted 90 days, spanned multiple projects and teams, and measured 11 different key performance indicators (KPIs). Although not reaching 50%+ efficiency gain as GitHub and GitClear reported, they've demonstrated positive results nonetheless. During their experiment, the average time to market decreased by 10% to 30% per project, sprint

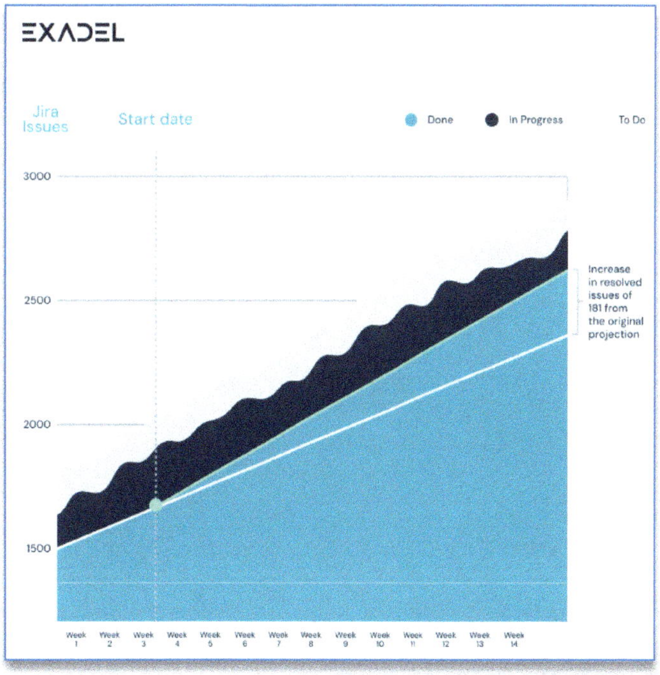

velocity increased by 11% to 27%, and technical debt dropped by 8% to 20%.[26,27,28]

Overall, the actual output improvement from using AI-supported coding averaged 18%, with 82.5% of experimenting developers feeling more productive when using those tools.

> *"All of these things are quite nice because they can be adopted when the time is right, when the technology is right, or when you're moving on to a new project. Maybe you don't use automated testing in this one, but you are using automated code generation, and vice versa. They're quite modular. You can keep plugging these in."*
>
> —Interview with Jamie Campbell
> Founder of MTX Solutions, Co-Founder of d3t Studio, ex-ATI (AMD), ex-Technical Director at THQ

Unity released two game-industry-specific AI tools in 2023. Muse is an AI platform that enables the generation of textures, characters, 3D assets, and even full games. It can code behavior commands in those assets as requested through chat commands. Sentis is a machine learning tool that analyzes your design preferences and generates game content automatically based on those preferences. The latter even learns from feedback and recommendations and adjusts accordingly. Feedback from the community is mitigated on the actual performance gain coming from these tools, but there's agreement that they are improving rapidly and could soon make essential impacts. The tools are better for art asset generation than for coding. They can also help with character rigging (the skeletal structure for animation).

[26] Time to market is the time it takes to develop a product from its initial design to a market release.

[27] Sprint velocity is how much content or tasks a team can deliver during one Agile sprint. Agile is a type of development and project management methodology which splits a project into phases.

[28] Technical debt, or code debt, is when a user writes fast, but bad, code, for the sake of a timed release, but that needs to be reworked and rewritten later on because of the lesser quality.

"J'ai encore l'impression que le coding, c'est un problème que les LLM font un beau travail avec. J'en suis convaincu. Les LLM ont été faites par des programmeurs, avec leur matière première; ils ont mis du code là-dedans. [...] Je trouve ça assez puissant ce que le GenAI peut faire au niveau du code."

AI translation: "I'm still under the impression that coding is a problem that LLMs solves well. I'm convinced of that. LLMs were made by programmers, with their raw material; their code. [...] I think it's pretty powerful what GenAI can do with code."

—Interview with Pierre-Paul Giroux
Vice-President Engineering A.I. at Unity

"Si tu commences à avoir des LLM qui respectent ton coding convention, t'es correct. [...] Je pense pas qu'on est encore rendu à faire une belle architecture complète de code, mais remplir une petite fonction, ça le fait quand même très bien. Puis ça, c'est time saving."

AI translation: "If you start getting LLMs that respect your coding convention, you're OK. [...] I don't think we've reached the point where we can create a beautiful, complete code architecture, but filling a small function does the trick just fine. And that's time saving."

-Interview with Pierre-Paul Giroux
Vice-President Engineering A.I. at Unity

Unreal doesn't offer a native AI tool at the moment, but it allows for plugins with AI capabilities. As for Unity, plugins primarily focus on art asset creation rather than game engineering.

Regarding external tools/plugins, Code Maestro claims a 50% efficiency and 100% productivity gain from using their tools for coding. [29] However, they can't provide accurate metrics; they used their tools on a low-complexity game, and their results haven't been third-party tested yet. The CEO stated that

[29] AI for Game Development: How Code Maestro is Making Waves, iLOGOS, https://ilogos.biz/ai-for-game-development-how-code-maestro-is-making-waves/, 15 May 2024

productivity gains vary between 32% and 100%, depending on the specific task. [30] This would translate to cost-efficiency gains of 24% to 50% per task, if applicable.

Other new AI tools are emerging, such as Buildbox. They can provide text input to programmed assets, but the quality remains limited. Developers primarily use them to create small, simple games or to prototype ideas, which they can then refine, largely without AI support.[31]

Examining larger consensus feedback from various development research studies, efficiency gains range from 10% to 30%, with the variation primarily based on the coder's experience level and, most importantly, on the complexity of the required task. According to Zippia, a career platform, becoming a software engineer typically takes 2-4 years, while becoming a game programmer usually takes 6-8 years, mainly because the latter is more complex and challenging.[32] From the same research, and for the sake of calculations in this analysis, the average game engineer earns $94,000 per year.

Based on this information, assuming most games are relatively complex, and to be conservative, we should accept a 10% efficiency gain from using AI coding support in games. This number aligns with feedback from various game developers gathered through interviews and other online reports.

Note that this research and the feedback received from interviews relied on tools that preceded OpenAI's o1. The latest GPT release, which claims a rise in coding performance from the 11th percentile with GPT-4 to 89th percentile with o1 and even 93rd percentile with o1-ioi, may indicate that we'll soon see a significant increase in coding applications and usage.[33]

---

[30] AI vs Crunch Time: How to Save 50% of Game Development Time with Code Maestro, Alexander Goldybin, Code Maestro, https://www.youtube.com/watch?v=U8k5jvZvDgo, 20 June 2024

[31] Buildbox AI, https://signup.buildbox.com/, visited 1 August 2024

[32] Game Programmer Vs Software Engineer, Zippia, https://www.zippia.com/game-programmer-jobs/game-programmer-vs-software-engineer-differences/, 5 April 2024

[33] Learning to Reason with LLMs: Coding, OpenAI, https://openai.com/index/learning-to-reason-with-llms/, 12 September 2024

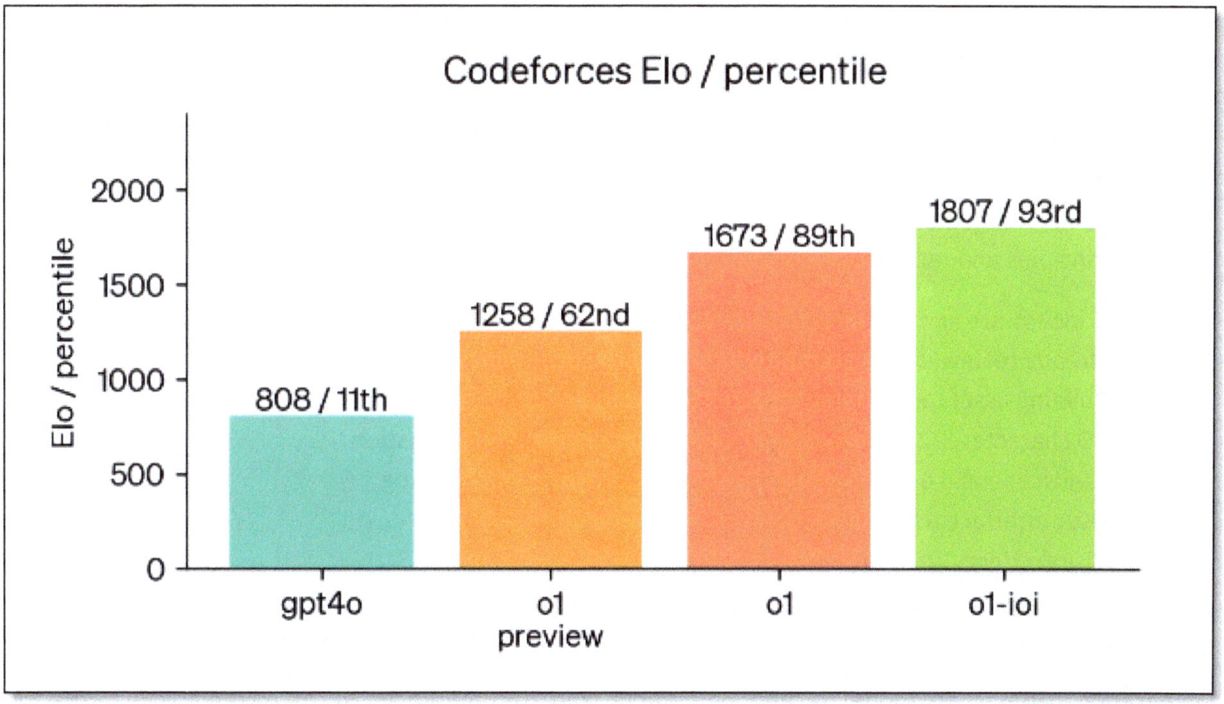

(Referencing why other analyses are only reaching 10-30% efficiency gains instead of the 75% he's seeing) ***"I think that it's because this analysis applies to companies where you are part of a team, and you have a role and you are in the same language, in which case I think this totally applies. [...] If I'm working in my comfortable environment, like writing game code in C Sharp, needing to write a character controller, then it would only be a 30% or so, because I already know how to make one. It would only use auto-complete or similar, and it would only speed things up a little."***

—Interview with Dylan Ebert, PhD
Developer Advocate Engineer, Hugging Face

"Some days I feel like AI is really helping. And then I spend hours debugging why my code is running slowly, and it's absolutely no help at all."

—Interview with Stephen Peacock
Director AI at 2K, Ex-Head of AI at AWS & Keywords

6.3 Visual Art Creation

In his book *The Art of Game Design*, Jesse Schell explains that games are constructed by the interrelation of four basic elements: mechanics, story, aesthetics, and technology.[34] Visual art creation is typically the bigger part of game aesthetics. Video game art encompasses conceptualizing, designing, and producing visual assets that enhance a game's overall aesthetic and immersive experience. From the initial concept art to the final in-game implementation, video game art demands a profound understanding of both artistic principles and technological limitations. This process mainly includes:

- Concept art and art direction, which are usually defined in the game design phase and were already reviewed and accounted for in a previous section of this research
- Building assets and adding textures & materials
- 3D character & 2D sprite design, modeling, rigging, and animation
- Landscape and environment creation, set dressing, and lighting
- User Interface (UI) design
- Visual Effects (VFX) design
- Cutscenes and cinematics

Technology is transforming game art creation through various techniques, including procedural generation, AI-assisted modeling and animation, and automated asset management (whether AI-supported or not).

> *"When I think about creativity, I think about two skills where one is searching for what is going to resonate with people or what you're trying to convey emotionally, or with experience, or just art, a vibe. And then you have the skill of actually producing it, generating it. And I think that the skill of producing is getting easier and easier."*
>
> —Interview with Dylan Ebert, PhD
> Developer Advocate Engineer, Hugging Face

Procedural generation in games has existed since the late 1970s. It's a method of creating data from algorithms instead of doing it manually. It's used in games to create large amounts of content automatically. Whilst it uses AI concepts, we won't explore its concepts and applications as its use is already widely adopted in game development, like for assets, items, characters, and environment creation.

To get an average result of the market, we've opted to build our analysis on examples of a large-sized high-end AA 3D game and AA 2D game, each with game development budgets of $10 million and $3.5 million, respectively.

---

[34] The Art of Game Design: A book of lenses, Jesse Schell, August 2008

On average, the art budget of a 3D AA game will vary between 25-30%. Using 28% as a benchmark for a high-end AAA game with a $10 million budget, we can extrapolate the following budget. Note that this is a rough estimate built from the feedback of industry experts. Actual budgets can vary greatly.

3D AA – Art budget	Cost	% of Art budget
Game assets	$700,000	25%
Character Design & Animation	$700,000	25%
Environment	$700,000	25%
User Interface	$280,000	10%
Visual Effects	$280,000	10%
Cinematics	$140,000	5%
Total	**$2,800,000**	**100%**

> *"I still think that you need to be a really skilled artist, regardless of what you're using, to find what will resonate with people. I think people are going to reorient their idea a bit around this."*
>
> -Interview with Dylan Ebert, PhD
> Developer Advocate Engineer, Hugging Face

Based on this budget and the efficiencies explained in the following sections, we can estimate a 68.7% cost-effectiveness in using AI for 3D art. This would result in a 219% productivity increase.

3D AA – Art cost	Human-only cost	AI-supplemented cost		Variation
		Human	AI	
Game assets	$700,000	$140,000	$0	-80.00%
Character Design & Animation	$700,000	$327,500	$83	-53.20%
Environment	$700,000	$182,000	$8,400	-72.80%
User Interface	$280,000	$56,000	$6,720	-77.60%
Visual Effects	$280,000	$70,000	$5,833	-72.92%
Cinematics	$140,000	$79,333	$622	-42.89%
Total	**$2,800,000**	**$854,833**	**$21,658**	**-68.70%**
Total	**$2,800,000**	**$876,492**		**-68.70%**
Total %	**100%**	**30.53%**	**0.77%**	**-68.70%**

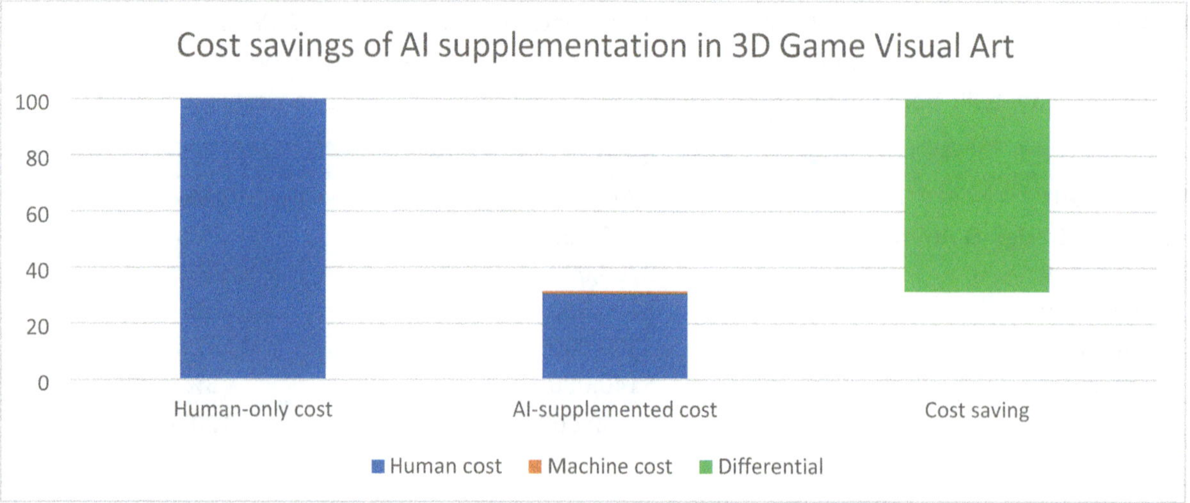

3D AA – Art output	Human Design	AI-supported Design
Output	1	3.1946
Productivity gains		**219.46%**

3D AA – Art output	Human-only Human cost & output	AI-supplemented Human cost & output	AI-supplemented Machine cost	AI-supplemented Machine output
Value 1	$2,800,000	$854,833.33	$21,658.22	$1,945,166.67
Ratio 1	100.00%	30.53%	0.77%	69.47%
Ratio AI-sup	319.46%	**97.53%**	2.47%	**221.93%**

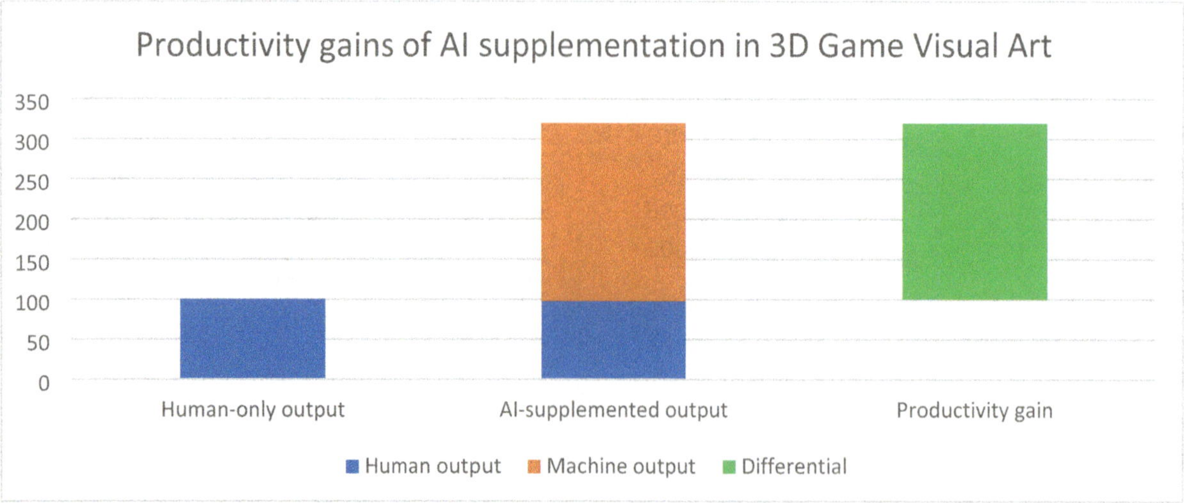

> *"On voit une grosse différence quand la personne avec laquelle on parle a compris, qu'en fait, ce (l'IA) n'est pas une fin en soi. Le fait de faire de la (Gen AI) 3D, de l'utiliser pour la 3D, c'est plutôt un outil qui te compacte, qui te rend beaucoup plus rapide sur certaines proportions de ton travail."*
>
> *AI translation: "You see a big difference when the person you're talking to has understood, that in fact, AI is not an end in itself. Using Gen AI for 3D makes you much faster on certain proportions of your work."*
>
> —Interview with Félix Balmonet
> Co-Founder & CEO, Chat3D

On average, the art budget of a 2D AA game is slightly less than a 3D one, at 25%. Using a $3.5 million budget for a high-end 2D AA as a benchmark, we get an art budget of $875,000. Below is the extrapolated budget. Again, note that this is a rough estimate built from the feedback of industry experts. Actual budgets can vary greatly.

2D AA – Art budget	Cost	% of Art budget
Game assets	$262,500	30%
Character Design & Animation	$218,750	25%
Environment	$175,000	20%
User Interface	$87,500	10%
Visual Effects	$87,500	10%
Cinematics	$43,750	5%
Total	**$875,000**	**100%**

Based on this budget and the efficiencies explained in the following sections, we can estimate a 71.5% cost-effectiveness in using AI in 2D art creation pipelines, and a corresponding 251% productivity gain.

2D AA – Art cost	Human-only cost	AI-supplemented cost		Variation
		Human	AI	
Game assets	$262,500	$52,500	$1,575	-79.40%
Character Design & Animation	$218,750	$68,750	$1,875	-67.71%
Environment	$175,000	$63,000	$1,680	-63.04%
User Interface	$87,500	$17,500	$2,100	-77.60%
Visual Effects	$87,500	$21,875	$1,823	-72.92%
Cinematics	$43,750	$15,750	$840	-62.08%
Total	**$875,000**	**$239,375**	**$9,893**	**-71.51%**
Total	**$875,000**	**$249,268**		**-71.51%**
Total %	**100%**	**27.36%**	**1.13%**	**-71.51%**

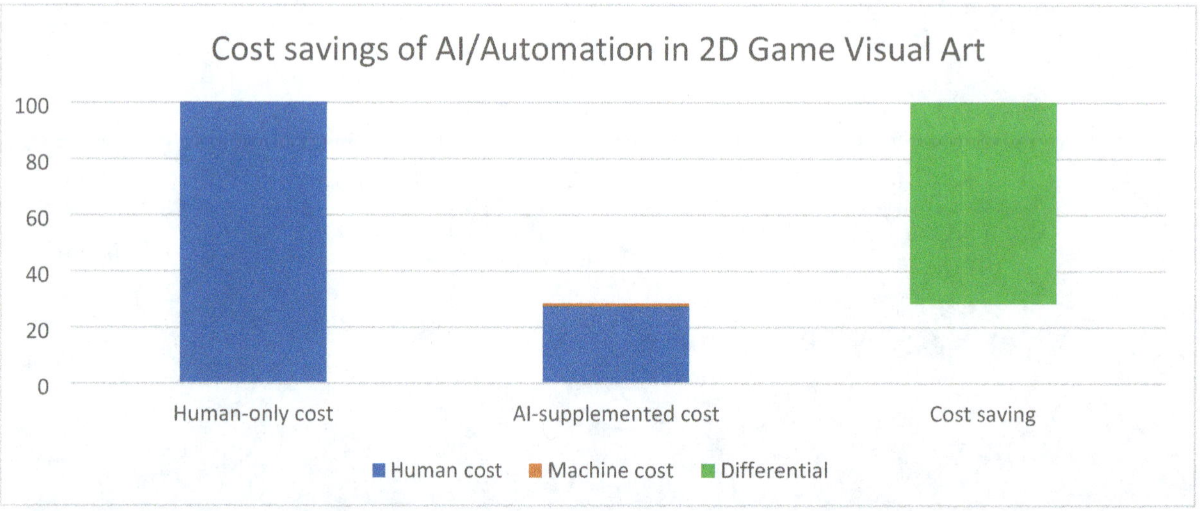

2D AA – Art output	Human Design	AI-supported Design
Output	1	3.5103
Productivity gains		**251.03%**

2D AA – Art output	Human-only Human cost & output	AI-supplemented Human cost & output	AI-supplemented Machine cost	AI-supplemented Machine output
Value 1	$875,000	$239,375	$9,893	$635,625
Ratio 1	100.00%	27.36%	1.13%	72.64%
Ratio AI-sup	351.03%	96.03%	3.97%	255.00%

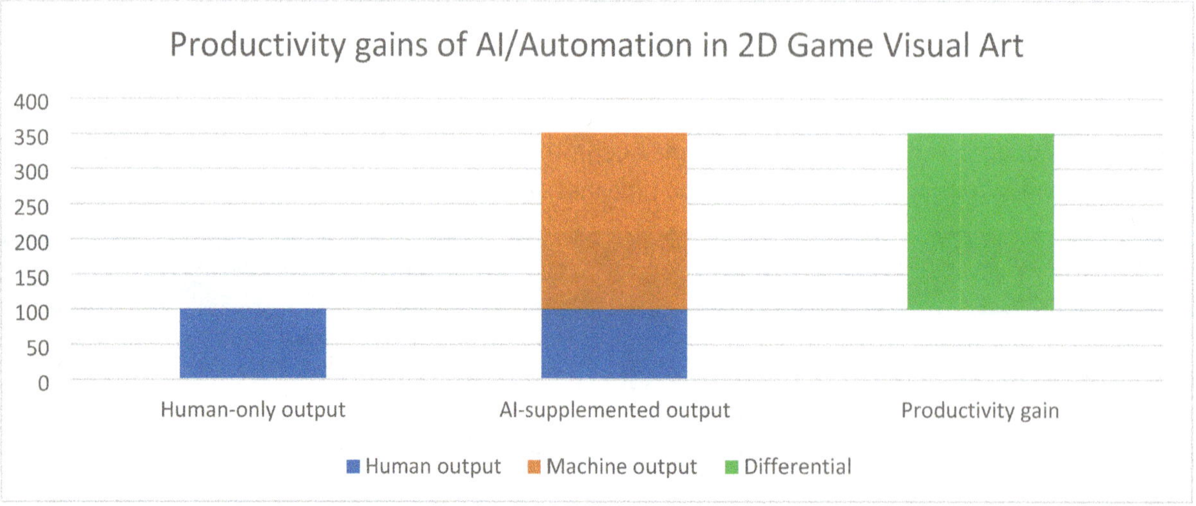

"Alors, quand on pense gain de productivité, au lieu de mettre un mois et demi, deux mois, à faire tous les assets, ils vont mettre deux, trois semaines. Mais en fait, ce qu'on observe aussi pas mal, c'est qu'il y a des studios qui gardent ces deux mois et qui, par contre, vont faire beaucoup plus d'assets. Le gain qualitatif, il est au niveau du fait qu'ils vont développer un univers qui sera beaucoup plus personnalisé. [...]
Pour le jeu vidéo, on constate davantage une massification du nombre d'objets créés qu'une production, qu'une réduction du temps en fait. "

AI translation: "When you think about productivity gains, instead of taking a month and a half to two months to do all the assets, they're going to take two or three weeks. What we're also seeing quite a lot are studios that keep those two months of work instead of scaling the work down and creating a lot more assets. The qualitative gain lies in the fact that they will be developing a much more personalized universe. [...] For video games, we're more frequently seeing an increase in the number of objects created, than a reduction in time."

—Interview with Félix Balmonet
Co-Founder & CEO, Chat3D

One might assume that 2D art, being simpler than 3D, would be easier to automate and would generate larger cost efficiencies and productivity gains by the use of AI. But our analysis shows similar gains in both fields. We assume that opportunity cost drives the lack of difference here. There's a higher gain to be had from automating costlier projects, like 3D ones, versus simpler 2D ones. We assume that the market and industry have invested in tool creation to automate those costlier projects, in a manner that aligns with their return on investment.

Game companies that have inserted AI into their art creation processes have reported similar and greater results. For example, Mighty Bear Games saw a 300% productivity gain after implementing AI in their 3D art pipeline. This would result in a potential 75% cost savings, which exceeds our own calculations. Some specialized artists quoted in this chapter achieved 80%+ cost efficiencies and 400%+ productivity gains. [35]

---

[35]Creating an AI-Assisted Art Tool to Optimize Efficiency in Game Art, Quinnie Cheuk, Medium, https://medium.com/mighty-bear-games/creating-an-ai-assisted-art-tool-to-optimize-efficiency-in-game-art-bf2a7c5e53ef, 2 August 2023

> *"Tasks that initially took an hour to complete were drastically reduced to just 10 minutes. Witnessing such incredible results was truly inspiring."*
>
> —Quinnie Cheuk, 3D animator, Mighty Bear Games

One important consideration is that AI art creation pipelines are more productive than standalone human ones; however, they may struggle to compete with the cost and speed of purchasing and utilizing art asset libraries, which are already competitively priced. Currently, AI is most beneficial in situations where no specific pre-existing asset can be used or purchased for a required task or project, whether because it doesn't exist, legal limitations apply, or other reasons. Both AI and art asset libraries could be used simultaneously, though, bringing up cost-effectiveness and productivity to even higher heights than what has been calculated and reported here. This is the case for most game art, including but not limited to: assets, characters, UI features, and VFX. It may also mean that an art pipeline, already streamlined by using asset libraries, may not get the same gains in cost or productivity as reported here.

> *"Être artiste aujourd'hui, c'est comprendre que les outils ressentent ce qu'on leur donne. Un artiste qui utilise l'IA parmi d'autres outils n'est pas un technicien : c'est quelqu'un qui s'en sert pour amplifier l'émotion."*
>
> *AI translation: "Being an artist today means understanding that tools feel what you give them. An artist who uses AI among other tools is not a technician: they are someone who uses it to amplify emotion."*
>
> —Interview with Frederic Vicaire
> Founder and Creative Director of art!equin agency

6.3.1 3D Assets, textures, and materials

Creating a 3D asset can cost between $40 and $2,000, with most costing around $500-600 for games.[36,37] The cost varies depending on the required complexity and level of detail.

Meshy offers text-to-3D, 2D image-to-3D, AI texturing, and text-to-voxel generation.[38] 3D asset and model exports can be done in many formats, including the most popular ones used in gaming engines and related art tools. The following is an example generated with 1 prompt and 1 refined model request. Each of these

[36] How Much Does it Cost to Create 3D Models?, Amélie Deltombe, https://sketchfab.com/blogs/enterprise/create-3d-models-cost, 20 October 2020

[37] A Guide to 2D Art & 3D Art Outsourcing Costs and Value, Pixune, https://pixune.com/blog/game-art-outsourcing-price/, 22 August 2024

[38] Meshy.AI, https://www.meshy.ai/, visited July 2024

steps costs 5 credits. The full generation costing 10 credits total. The platform operates on a monthly subscription model, where the cost of limited plans ranges from $0.12 to $0.20 per asset (for 10 credits). An unlimited plan is also available at $120 per month. The output isn't perfect, but for 20 cents per asset, the results are excellent. It provides approximately 75-80% of the work done at a fraction of the price, with only final review and editing needed by a game artist. The production time of less than a minute for the below is also quite rapid compared to the usual 20-40 hours per detailed asset, and 60+ hours for higher detailed ones. The turnaround time is improved greatly as well. The art creator and other relevant creative stakeholders often spend 2-10 weeks creating assets due to the back-and-forth communication required.

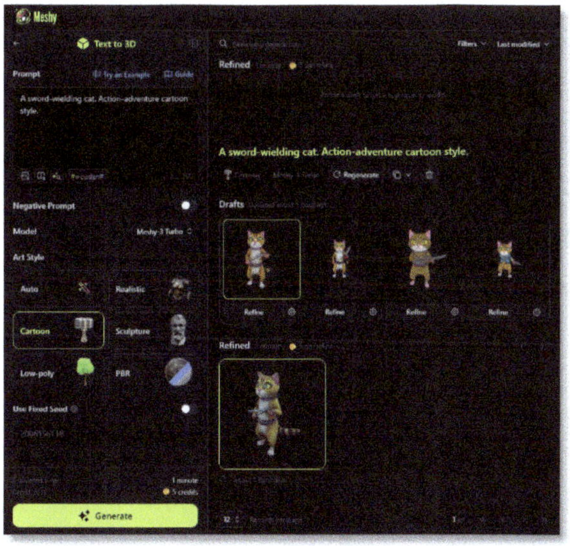

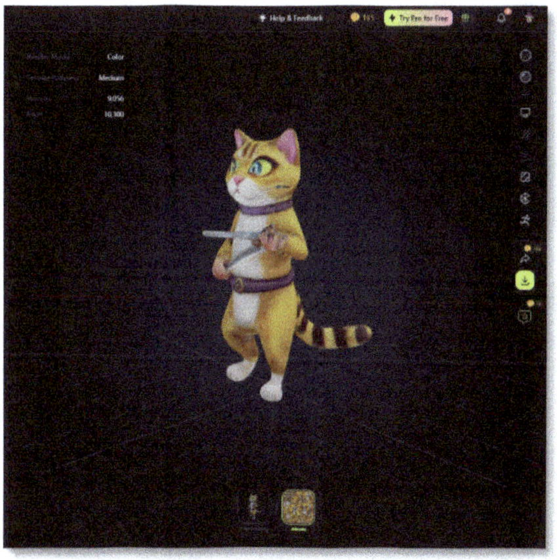

"Pour faire du prototypage, leurs designers vont faire quelque chose en 2D dessiné à la main. Ils vont le passer en 3D, vont le mettre en VR et le resculpter en 3D. C'est une étape qui n'existait pas avant. C'est vraiment quelque chose de nouveau qui s'est créé."

AI translation: "To do prototyping, their designers will draw something in 2D by hand. They'll take it to 3D, put it in VR and resculpt it in 3D. It's a step that didn't exist before. It's really something new that's been created."

—Interview with Félix Balmonet
Co-Founder & CEO, Chat3D

“Si tu donnes ça à un artiste 3D traditionnel, pour ce qu'on a fait, il mettait environ 4 heures. Et avec notre solution, il mettait moins d'une heure. [...] On est au moins 75% plus rapide. Même parfois jusqu'à 90%.”

AI translation: "If you give that to a traditional 3D artist, for what we did, he'd take about 4 hours. With our solution, it took less than an hour. [...] We're at least 75% faster. Sometimes even up to 90%."

—Interview with Félix Balmonet
Co-Founder & CEO, Chat3D

Luma Labs’ Genie tool can generate even more accurate 3D asset renditions and is currently offered for free.[39] Below are self-generated examples.

Here are other rendered examples created and shared by users on the online platform.

[39] Genie, Luma Labs, https://lumalabs.ai/genie, visited July 2024

"L'endroit où les outils deviennent intéressants, c'est au niveau du remixing. Le meilleur exemple que je peux donner pour des sprites et des textures, c'est de faire un seasonal update. Exemple, c'est l'Halloween, un DLC skin sort pour Halloween. C'est là que Generative AI est incroyablement puissante. Tu laisses la créativité aux gens, et tu utilise l'AI pour la productivité."

AI translation: "Where the tools become interesting is in remixing. A good example of sprites and textures is a seasonal update. For example, a DLC skin is released for Halloween. This is where Generative AI is incredibly powerful. You leave creativity to people, and use AI for productivity."

—Interview with Pierre-Paul Giroux
Vice-President Engineering A.I. at Unity

For $1 per capture, Luma Labs also offers Video to 3D via their Luma API.[40] It can create high-quality, photorealistic 3D assets and environments in minutes. It needs little to no editing from an artist, depending on the desired detail, essentially automating 95%+ of the work historically done by hand.

These are only 3 examples, where many others now exist and are available via online platforms or through downloadable APIs. In any case, these three examples demonstrate

[40] Luma API, Luma Labs, https://lumalabs.ai/luma-api, visited July 2024

game art creation cost efficiencies varying between approximately 75% and 95%, technology costs varying between $0 (free) and $1 per asset, and final productivity gains varying between +300% and +1,823%.

3D asset creation	Human-only cost	Meshy-supported cost	Genie-supported cost	Luma-supported cost
Human cost	$500	$125	$100	$25
AI/Tool cost	$0	$0.20	$0	$1
Total	**$500**	**$125.20**	**$100**	**$26**
Cost efficiency		**-74.96%**	**-80.00%**	**-94.80%**

3D asset creation	Human-only output	Meshy-supported output	Genie-supported output	Luma-supported output
Output	1	3.9936	5	18.2308
Productivity gain		**299.36%**	**400.00%**	**1823.08%**

For the sake of this analysis and to remain conservative, we will consider the Genie-supported values above in the calculations of efficiency and productivity for the AI-supported visual arts.

Of note, but not added to the above calculations or considerations, is Kaedim. Kaedim is an art service provider (business process outsourcing, or BPO) that uses an internally built and proprietary AI platform to generate 3D game art within a "human-in-the-loop" and final human review process.[41] Through four client-backed business cases, Kaedim demonstrates cost efficiency gains ranging from 75% to 95%, resulting in productivity gains between 300% and 1900%.[42] The tools are not accessible by their clients, though, and human-to-AI work ratios are not visible to us.

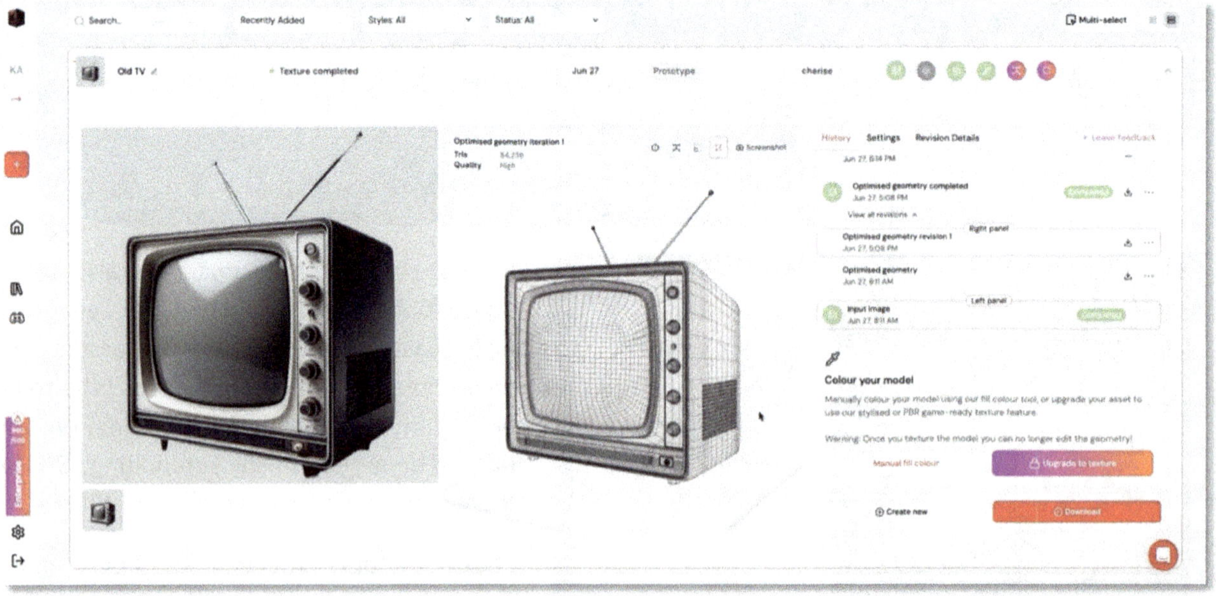

[41] About Us, Kaedim, https://www.kaedim3d.com/about-us, visited July 2024
[42] Case Studies, Kaedim, https://www.kaedim3d.com/case-study, visited July 2024

6.3.2 3D Character design, modeling, rigging, and animation

Creating a 3D character for games, including rigging (articulation placement) and animation (movements) can cost between $3,000 and $16,000, with an average of $7,000 for games.[43] The cost varies depending on the required complexity, level of detail, and the number of revisions or rush fees. The main cost differences between creating a standard 3D asset and a character are the rigging costs and the animation ones.

3D Character – Human Design	Low-end	Mid-range	High-end
Design (3D Asset Creation)	$500	$2,000	$5,000
Rigging	$500	$750	$1,000
Animation	$2,000	$3,500	$5,000
Revisions & Other costs	$0	$750	$5,000
Total	**$3,000**	**$7,000**	**$16,000**

Reallusion's Actorcore AccuRIG is a free 3D character AI-assisted auto-rigging tool.[44] It achieves approximately 85% accuracy, requiring minimal effort to review and complete the process, which users can do within the same tool once the automated rigging is finished. Most models needing more effort are amorphous and/or asymmetrical. Reallusion offers AccuRIG for free, potentially as a loss-leader for their other products and services.

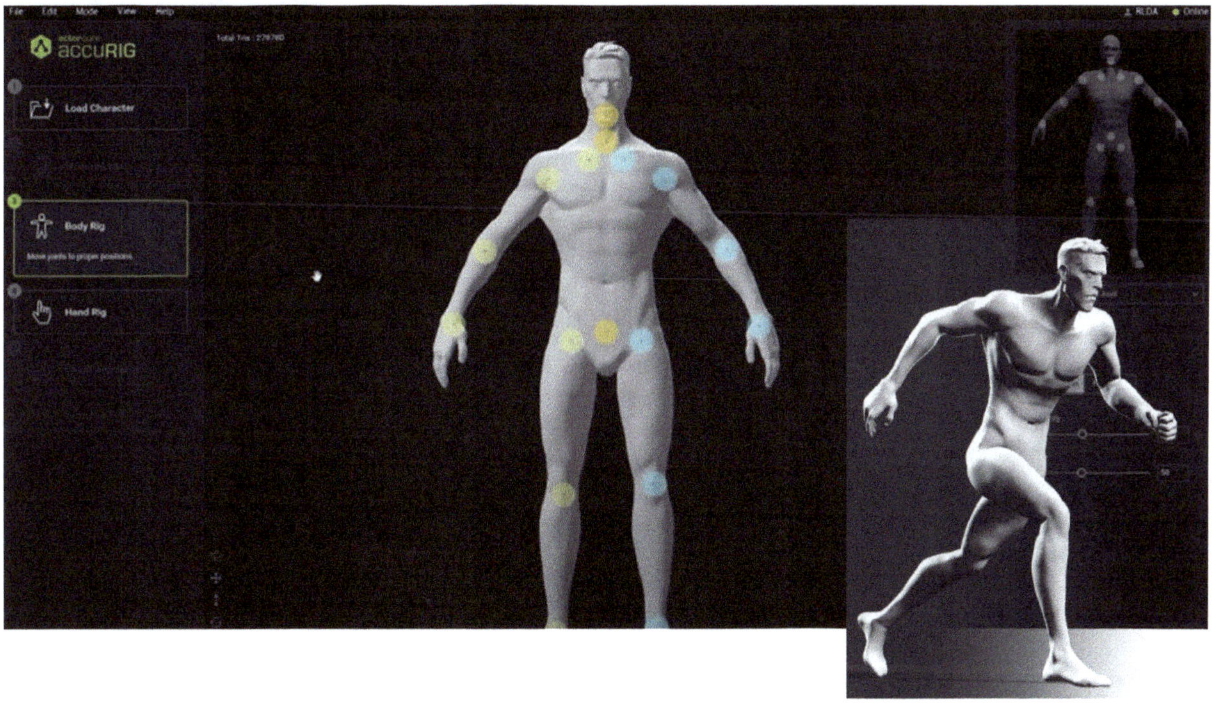

[43] How much does a character design cost? How to choose the right character design company, Juego Studios, https://www.juegostudio.com/blog/character-design-cost, 19 June 2023

[44] AccuRIG, Actorcore (Reallusion), https://actorcore.reallusion.com/auto-rig/accurig, visited July 2024

Another company, Anything World, offers AI-supported rigging and animation. If entered correctly and falling into their predefined model categories, the output achieves a high level of accuracy. It has limitations, though, and some difficulties with asymmetrical entities or anything that doesn't fall within their preconceived models. It's also better suited for simpler models; compared to AccuRIG, this tool isn't able to rig hands and fingers. Regarding the AI-supported animation, although it is currently present, it is still in development. Those automated models produce a limited and not fully functional outcome. In both rigging and animation, although the automation is limited, the efforts it automates can still easily reduce the amount of manual work by about 50%.[45]

They offer limited and unlimited credit/model plans. For limited plans, the cost of rigging and animating a model ranges from $0.625 to $0.833.

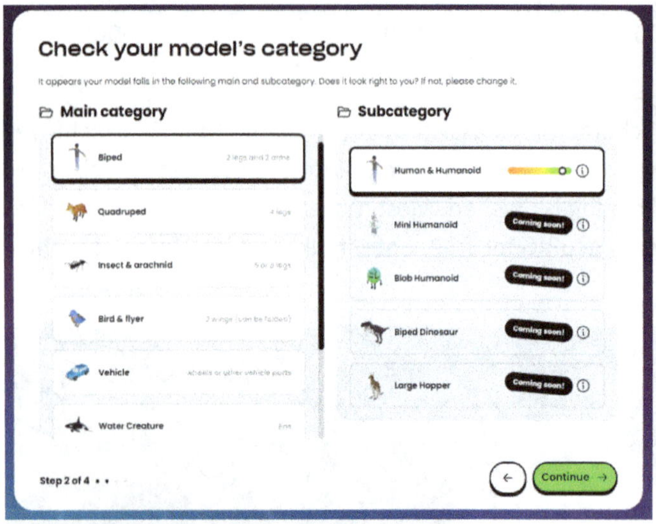

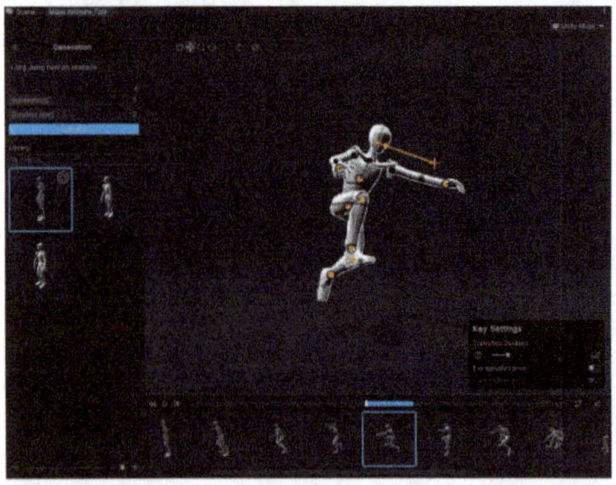

Notably, Unity's Muse Animate AI tool provides AI-assisted animations for pre-rigged models.[46] Currently, feedback on its quality is mixed. Still, it is agreed that it saves time for animators. The amount of time and cost saved, though, doesn't seem to match current animation packages being sold online, and they can simply be downloaded, imported, and applied to a project.

Other notable AI tools include OpenPose, MocapNet, Rokoko Studio, Plask, and DeepMotion, which can use video recordings and a pre-rigged humanoid model to automatically animate the model from video recordings.

[45] 3D Animation and Automated Rigging, Anything World, https://anything.world/, visited July 2024
[46] Muse, Unity, https://unity.com/products/muse, visited August 2024

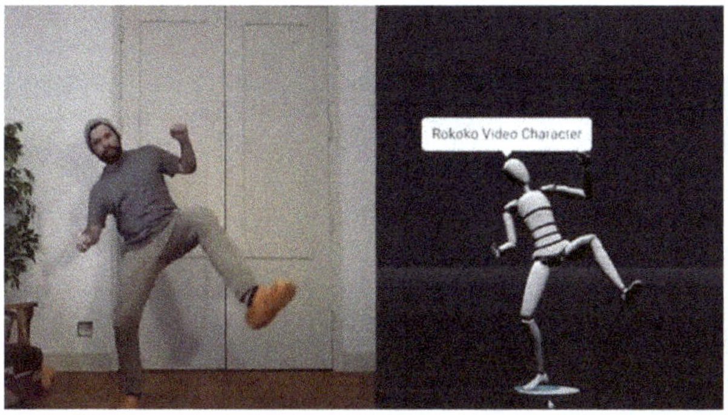

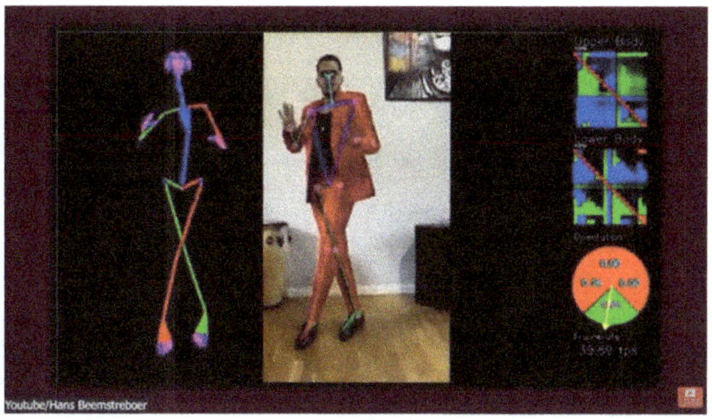

Another very interesting tool is Wonder Dynamics' Wonder Studio. It can automatically animate, light, and compose computer graphics, but is currently focused on live-action scenes, mainly for the movie industry. We assume it's only a matter of time until this type of tool becomes more accessible and applicable to the game industry, especially considering that outputs can already be created in Unreal and Blender, and that Epic Games is an investor.

While these tools cover main rigging and animation, some characters in certain games may also require separate face animation. Nvidia's Audio2Face manages to animate most pre-rigged faces via audio files within its Omniverse tool, which greatly reduces the animator's workload.

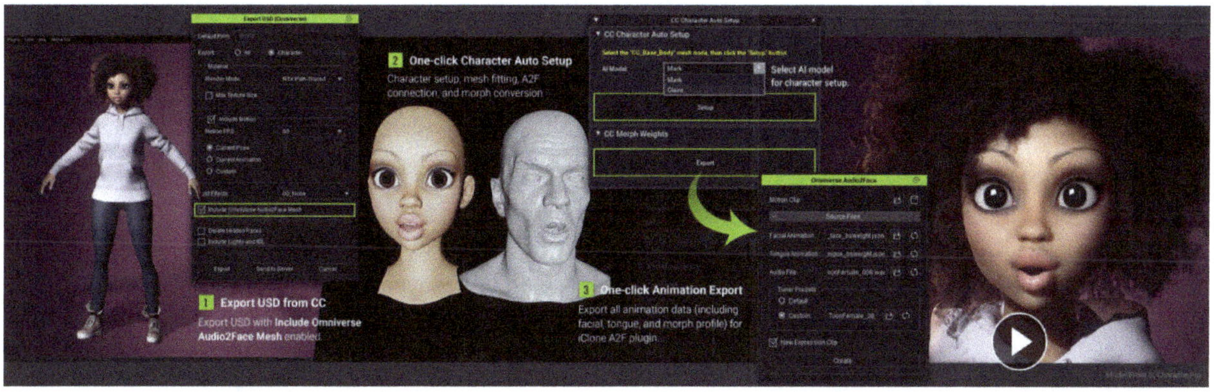

Using these tools alongside those presented in the previous section would enable cost efficiencies of 28 to 53%, resulting in productivity gains of 38 to 114%. As a caveat, note that we conduct the following analysis on a mid-range AA 3D character creation that does not require extensive facial animation. Design costs are based on the previous subsection's calculations.

3D Character (Mid-Range)	Human-only cost	AccuRIG-supported cost	AA-supported cost
Design (3D Asset Creation)[47]	$2,000	$400	$400
Rigging	$750	$112.50	$375
Animation	$3,500	$3,500	$1,750
Revisions & Other costs	$750	$750	$750
AI/Tool cost	$0	$0	$0.83
Total	**$7,000**	**$4,762.50**	**$3,275.83**
Cost efficiency		**-31.96%**	**-53.20%**

[47] Using tools and analysis from 3D Asset Creation section.

3D Character (Mid-Range)	Human-only output	AccuRIG-supported output	AA-supported output
Output	1	1.4698	2.1369
Productivity gains		**46.98%**	**113.69%**

> *"In 3D, I'm kind of frustrated with the gap between research and application, especially since I'm involved with both of them, and I can see where each side does not see the other one. Especially researchers don't understand what 3D artists do, or what they need, or what's useful for them. [...] For a long time, there's been this frustrating thing where researchers are incentivized to have results on paper that look better, or they have a benchmark score that is higher based on how similar it is to the real image. But they don't care, historically, at all about topology, or UV maps, or materials, or any of these things that are critically important for artists. [...] I think there are some lessons that can be learned in that there should be more focus on what is actually useful for artists. [...] It's improving with companies like Tencent, which has been making really good strides in 3D AI because they actually use it as well as develop it."*
>
> —Interview with Dylan Ebert, PhD
> Developer Advocate Engineer, Hugging Face

6.3.3 3D Landscape and environment creation, set dressing, and lighting

Creating a 3D environment for games, including modeling and texturing, usually costs between $1,500 and $10,000, with most costing around $5,000. As always, costs vary per required complexity and level of detail.

When examining the process of building a 3D environment, it typically involves the superposition of multiple 3D assets. As such, we can assume that the efforts are primarily focused on creating those assets first and foremost, and then integrating them into an environment.

As mentioned, for $1 per capture, Luma Labs offers Video to 3D capabilities through its Luma API. It can generate high-quality, photorealistic environments in just a few minutes, automating most of the work. The tool seems to be able to handle assets better than complex environments, though but can still reduce necessary efforts by ≈80%.

Promethean AI is an AI-powered asset management and environment-building tool. It creates environments from a pre-existing library of assets using text prompts.[48] Users report up to 10 times faster environment creation if the assets are pre-existing and cataloged.[49] Based on industry feedback, the tool appears to be 50% as effective for environmental creation and 10% effective for the overall art production pipeline.[50] Their professional plan costs $60 per month. They also offer an enterprise plan, which is custom-priced.

Using Luma Labs' video-to-3D capabilities, or the other 3D asset tools mentioned, along with Promethean AI to create environments from a studio's own assets, would result in a 72.8% cost savings and a 268% boost in productivity.

3D Environment	Human-only cost	AI-supplemented cost
Design (3D Asset Creation)	$4,000	$800
Superposition & lighting	$1,000	$500
AI/Tool cost	$0	$60[51]
Total	**$5,000**	**$1,360**
Cost efficiency		**-72.8%**

3D Environment	Human-only output	AI-supplemented output
Output	1	3.6765
Productivity gains		**267.65%**

[48] Promethean AI, https://www.prometheanai.com/, visited July 2024
[49] AI World Building, Promethean AI, https://www.prometheanai.com/ai-world-building, visited July 2024
[50] AI asset management, Promethean AI, https://www.prometheanai.com/asset-management, visited July 2024
[51] 1 full month license for conservative calculation. Actual value likely much less than that.

"Il y a 1 an, personne n'utilisait la Gen AI. [...]
Maintenant je crois que moins de 5% des artistes l'utilise. [...]
Pour le (Gen AI) 3D, la majorité des gens ne savent même pas que ca existe."

AI translation: "A year ago, nobody was using Gen AI. [...]
Now I believe less than 5% of artists use it. [...]
Most people don't even know that (Gen AI) 3D exists.

—Interview with Félix Balmonet
Co-Founder & CEO, Chat3D

6.3.4 2D Assets, textures, and materials

Creating a 2D asset can cost between $40 and $800, with most costing around $200 for games. Cost varies per required complexity and level of detail.

Using the techniques described previously with tools like DALL-E and Midjourney, creators can remove 80% or more of the manual efforts from the creation process.

2D Asset Creation (100 assets)	Human-only cost	AI-supplemented cost
Human cost	$20,000	$4,000
AI/Tool cost	$0	$120[52]
Total	**$20,000**	**$1,120**
Cost efficiency		**-79.4%**

2D Asset Creation (100 assets)	Human-only output	AI-supplemented output
Output	1	4.8544
Productivity gains		385.44%

"Pour les artistes 2D, je pense que plus de 80% l'ont utilisé au moins une fois."

AI translation: "I believe that over 80% of 2D artists have used it at least once."
-Interview with Félix Balmonet
Co-Founder & CEO, Chat3D

[52] Costliest monthly price of Midjourney.

Of note, but not applied to this analysis, is the use of AI post-editing tools like Magnific.[53] These tools use AI to generate, fill and add to images. It can enhance positively image generated through DALL-E and Midjourney, and even human-generated ones. Below are before and after upscaled pictures. The processed picture, on the right, contains better and more details, and is outputted at a higher resolution than the original picture, on the left.

6.3.5 2D Sprite design, modeling, rigging, and animation

Creating a 2D game character, including rigging (articulation placement) and animation (movements), can cost between $350 and $3,900, with an average of $1,400 for games. The cost varies depending on the required complexity, level of detail, and the number of revisions or rush fees. Similarly to 3D, the main cost differences between creating a standard 2D asset and a character are the rigging costs, if any, and the animation ones.

2D Character – Human Design	Low-end	Mid-range	High-end
Design (2D Asset Creation)	$250	$600	$1,000
Rigging[54]	$0	$0	$800
Animation	$100	$400	$800
Revisions & Other costs	$0	$200	$1,300
Total	**$350**	**$1,400**	**$3,900**

[53] Magnific AI – The magic image upscaler & enhancer, Magnific AI, https://magnific.ai/#games, visited August 2024
[54] Rigging is not necessarily needed for 2D animation.

Using Midjourney or DALL-E to create the initial design and a sprite animation sheet can shave off over 80% of the manual work for that first step. Some self-experimental examples below.

Prompt: "*Create a sprite sheet of a cartoon cat wielding a sword, 9 sprite image per picture, following the same sword movement, all facing the same side*"

Output:

Midjourney 6.1 Picture 1

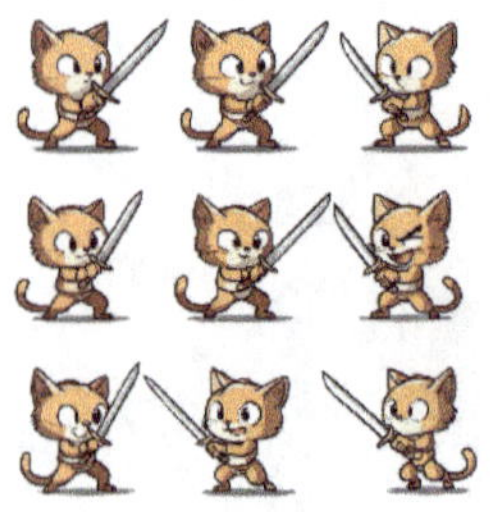

Midjourney 6.1 Picture 2

DALL-E 3 Picture 1

DALL-E 3 Picture 2

Midjourney6.1 Picture 3

Midjourney 6.1 Picture 4

DALL-E 3 Picture 3

DALL-E 3 Picture 4

> *"A less experienced artist might be able to tweak a model and get a decent result. But for a skilled artist, the experience can be frustrating. It's like trying to backseat-drive your own creative process."*
>
> —Interview with Stephen Peacock
> Director AI at 2K, Ex-Head of AI at AWS & Keywords

Unity's Muse offers AI sprite generation options, including the ability to provide your own data or style for learning purposes. The feedback the game art community has been balanced between positive and negative at the moment, as the output from the tool has been hit-and-miss in its current early days. It is improving rapidly, though.

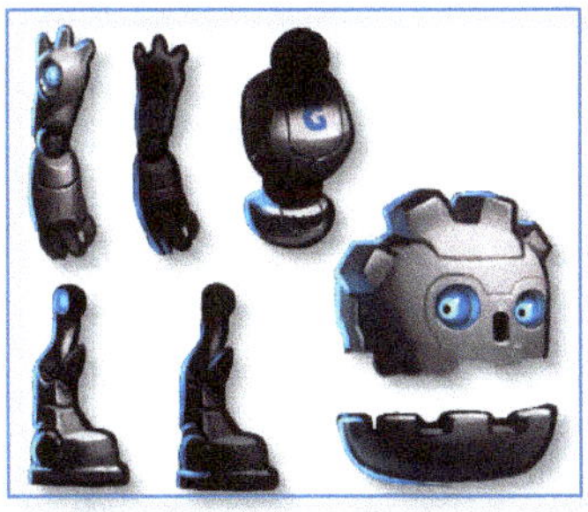

Rigging isn't always used in 2D games. When used, it often uses a different form of rigging than 3D. A sprite is often divided into its constituent parts, which are then combined in separate steps to simplify and facilitate animations. Rigging this way negates additional distortion between shapes (body parts) that could look unnatural. On the left, an example demonstrating the process in Godot, a free open-source game engine. Although present in some games, this process is more commonly used in movie and cartoon animation.

Kestrel Moon's Creature tool's Smart AI Auto Rig is capable of automating some basic rigging. While this can save a little bit of time, the option is limited to humanoid characters only. One advantage, though, is that a T-pose or symmetrical pose isn't necessary to achieve satisfactory results. The 2D picture of a fighter on the right shows an example of this.[55]

> *"As these tools mature, users will gain much more control. Right now, prompting a language model or generating a single image with Stable Diffusion can feel like rolling the dice. That won't always be the case."*
>
> —Interview with Stephen Peacock
> Director AI at 2K, Ex-Head of AI at AWS & Keywords

Of note, but outside the scope of this research because of its limited exportable format for game integration, is Meta's Animated Drawings AI demo.[56] The tool is still in its infancy, but it can do a decent job at both auto-rigging and providing animation previews from animation presets.

---

[55] Creature: The Automated animation Tool, Kestrel Moon, https://www.kestrelmoon.com/creature/more_info_2.html, visited August 2024

[56] Animated Drawings, Meta, https://sketch.metademolab.com/, visited July 2024

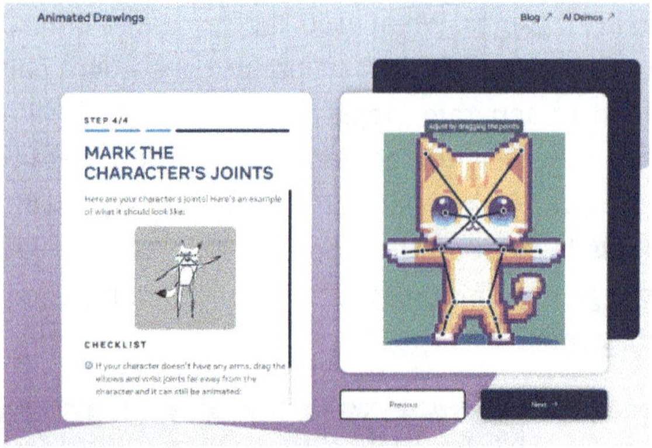

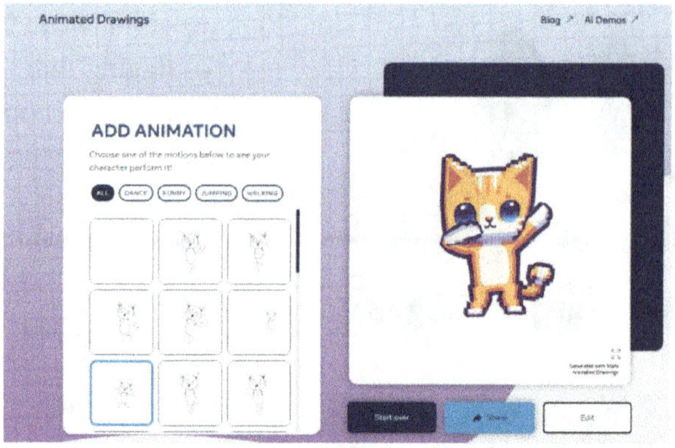

Animating these rigs can be done via AI generation. It is still very early days, and the automated process still has a long way to go. Currently, it is more cost-effective to start by purchasing animation packages than to attempt to leverage AI for these animations, considering the amount of manual work required for corrections afterward.

Frame-by-frame individual image animated sprites are a common way to make character animations in 2D games. They are less flexible than rigged animation, but can require less effort for predefined actions in a simple game, especially for "pixel art" or lower-definition graphics games. Below is an example from Godot.[57]

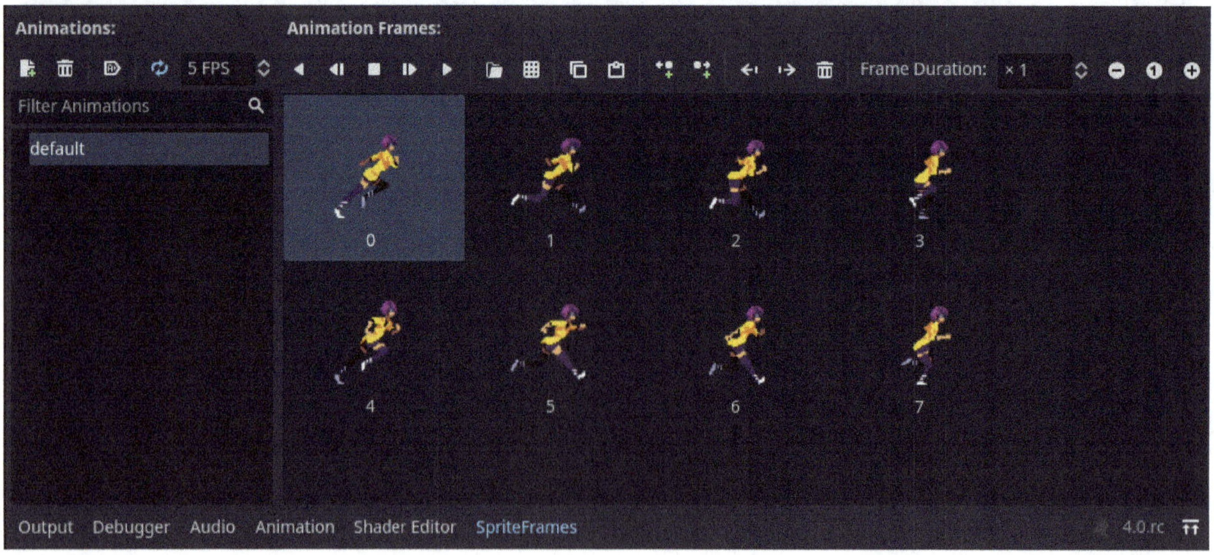

This process connects well with the sprite sheet process demonstrated with DALL-E and Midjourney previously, where, if prompted properly, most of the base work can be done via AI. Notably, however, this process wouldn't utilize rigging at all and may not be suitable for all types of games. Like other AI-supported methods, it would require manual editing for quality control before being integrated into the animation.

---

57 2D sprite animation, Godot Engine 4.3 Documentation, Godot, https://docs.godotengine.org/en/stable/tutorials/2d/2d_sprite_animation.html, visited August 2024

Using the techniques mentioned above for 2D character creation would achieve a 68% reduction in costs and a 210% increase in productivity compared to a human-only approach.

2D Character (Mid-Range)	Human-only cost	AI-supplemented cost
Design (2D Asset Creation)	$600	$120
Rigging & Animation	$600	$120
Revisions & Other costs	$200	$200
AI/Tool cost	$0	$12[58]
Total	**$1,400**	**$452**
Cost efficiency		-67.71%

2D Character (Mid-Range)	Human-only output	AI-supplemented output
Output	1	3.0973
Productivity gains		**+209.73%**

6.3.6 2D Landscape and environment creation, set dressing, and lighting

As in 3D, creating a 2D environment typically involves the superposition of multiple 2D assets. As such, we can assume that the efforts are primarily focused on creating those assets and then arranging them within an environment. And again, most of these assets could be generated initially from AI.

Even when assuming a fully manual process to superimpose those assets in an environment, using AI for this process would generate a 63% cost efficiency and a 171% productivity gain.

2D Environment	Human-only cost	AI-supplemented cost
Design (2D Asset Creation)	$1,000	$200
Superposition & lighting	$250	$250
AI/Tool cost	$0	$12[59]
Total	**$1,250**	**$462**
Cost efficiency		**-63.04%**

2D Environment	Human-only output	AI-supplemented output
Output	1	2.7056
Productivity gains		**170.56%**

[58] Assuming 10 characters and 1 month worth of the priciest license. Overestimated cost for analysis purposes.
[59] Assuming 10 environment and 1 month worth of the priciest license. Overestimated cost for analysis purposes.

> *"The obvious advantage is efficiency and iteration. That was the first thing that occurred to me, especially when I started seeing the image models coming out as artists need to iterate."*
>
> —Interview with Liza Wood
> Principal Group Program Manager – Data & AI Leader at Microsoft
> Ex-Disney/WB Games/Behavior/EA

> *"Plus que les outils vont être puissants, plus qu'on va pouvoir enlever tout ce qui est mundane et répétitif dans les processus."*
>
> *AI translation: "The more powerful the tools are going to be, the more we'll be able to remove everything mundane and repetitive from the processes."*
>
> —Interview with Pierre-Paul Giroux
> Vice-President Engineering A.I. at Unity

6.3.7 3D & 2D User interface design

User interface (UI) design currently costs between $100 and $400 per UI page (screen) with an average of $250 per page. These could be starting menu pages, pause menu pages, and UI overlays. As an example, a game with 20 menu and UI overlay pages would cost, on average, $5,000 before reviews and editing.

Most user interfaces are 2D. Standard AI image generators can easily create these images. As with previous examples, I've self-generated the below with Midjourney and DALL-E. To note, to achieve an appropriate result, I had to go through two prompts on DALL-E and four prompts on Midjourney, reiterating the need for an experienced prompt engineer to obtain the desired results from the machine.

While the team needs to do some work to finalize the product, they can easily reduce the ideation and design efforts required to create it by 80% by using AI image generation. Per the following calculations, using these tools for this UI creation would result in cost efficiencies of 77.6% and productivity gains of 346.43%.

DALL-E 3 final prompt: "*start menu User Interface images for a 2d video game, cute cartoony style, for a game featuring a sword-wielding cat fighting dragons*"

Midjourney 6.1 final prompt: "*start menu User Interface images for a 2d video game, with relevant game start buttons and icons, cute cartoony style, for a game featuring a sword-wielding cat fighting dragons*"

Output:

Midjourney 6.1 Picture 1

Midjourney 6.1 Picture 2

DALL-E 3 Picture 1

DALL-E 3 Picture 2

Midjourney6.1 Picture 3

Midjourney 6.1 Picture 4

DALL-E 3 Picture 3

DALL-E 3 Picture 4

User Interface	Human-only cost	AI-supplemented cost
Human cost	$5,000	$1,000
AI/Tool cost	$0	$120[60]
Total	**$5,000**	**$1,120**
Cost efficiency		**-77.6%**

User Interface	Human-only output	AI-supplemented output
Output	1	4.4643
Productivity gains		346.43%

6.3.8 Visual effects

Game visual effects (VFX) are computer-generated elements that improve game experience and realism. They create immersive and dynamic game environments by adding depth and atmosphere. VFX can include particle effects, lighting effects, explosions, fluid simulations, and more.

The costs of VFX vary significantly, ranging from $1,000 per VFX minute to $100,000 or more. Budgets typically fall between $2,000 and $10,000 for small, simple projects, while major blockbuster projects can exceed $100,000,000. A typical game studio VFX cost will be around $10,000 per minute. An average game VFX project (for a low- to mid-tier game) will cost approximately $60,000. [61]

---

60 Costliest monthly price of Midjourney. Actual costs likely lower.

61 3D VFX Cost + Influencing Factors, Nazanin Shahbazi, https://pixune.com/blog/3d-vfx-cost/, 22 August 2024

VFX Type	Low-end minute cost	High-end minute cost
Basic	$1,000	$2,000
Intermediate	$2,000	$5,000
Advanced	$5,000	$20,000
Highly complex	$20,000	$100,000+

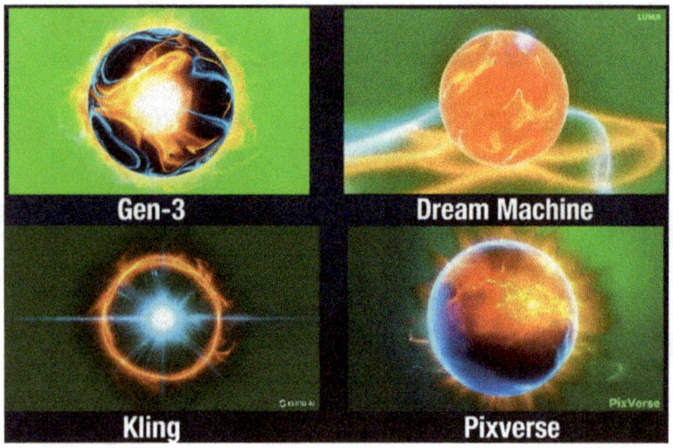

There are growing business cases for utilizing AI tools like Runway to generate visual effects (VFX). Here is an example by Futurepedia's Kevin Hutson. He generated an animated plasma ball on Runway Gen-3, Luma's Dream Machine, Kling AI, and PixVerse AI.[62] One anonymous artist reports that, with AI support, they can create in 2 days what used to take them 8. Another advised that what used to take them a week's worth of effort now takes a day or less, including correcting any errors AI might have introduced. Essentially, 75% and 80% cost efficiencies, and respective 300% and 400% productivity gains.

"The most fascinating was watching art directors debate AI, because you can see the spectrum. On one side, the ones saying: yes, this is a tool, this is going to enable me to iterate, we're embracing it, this can expand my creativity. And on the other end of the spectrum: no, it's not perfect, so therefore I'm not going to adopt it."

—Interview with Liza Wood
Principal Group Program Manager – Data & AI Leader at Microsoft
Ex-Disney/WB Games/Behavior/EA

Assuming a team of 10 artists working for 1 month on a project (or similar permutation like 1 artist working for 10 months), even when taking in the more conservative of the 2 case scenarios, and the costliest Runway paid plan, we still end up with a 73% cost efficiency and 269% productivity gain.

---

[62] Generative VFX with Runway Gen-3 | Create AI Visual Effects, Kevin Hutson, Futurepedia, https://www.youtube.com/watch?v=pGEW7AKcLrg, 19 August 2024

VFX	Human-only cost	AI-supplemented cost
Human cost	$60,000	$15,000
AI/Tool cost	$0	$1,250[63]
Total	**$60,000**	**$15,125**
Cost efficiency		**-72.92%**

VFX	Human-only output	AI-supplemented output
Output	1	3.6923
Productivity gains		**269.23%**

6.3.9 Cutscenes and cinematics

Game cinematics, also known as in-game non-interactive movies or cutscenes, are sequences that appear within the game. People use them for storytelling, world-building, and transitioning between scenes or levels within a game. They can be pre-rendered or rendered in real-time. Pre-rendered means they were built outside the game and then imported in. Real-time rendered means they were built within the game using its engine, environments, and asset animations. In addition to the visual arts portion, they often include design costs, such as scene and script writing, as well as audio costs, including voiceovers, sound effects, and music, which we'll review in the following production analysis section.

Whether it's long cinematics, short cutscenes, or marketing trailers, costs can vary significantly, ranging from $1,000 to $250,000 per movie minute, or more, including all non-visual expenses. The top of the bracket is usually attributable to some of the costlier high-end AAA games. If we look solely at the costs of game cinematics visual arts, we see that they average $10,000 to $15,000 per minute for 3D renditions. 2D pre-rendered rendition costs range from $1,000 to $10,000 per minute, with an average of $3,000 per minute. 2D real-time rendition costs range between $500 and $2,000 per minute, with an average of $1,250 per minute. [64,65]

Regarding pre-rendered movies, current AI tool capabilities are somewhat limited and are hardly usable in games at present. Video Gen AI models appear to have more ease with realistic renditions, which makes sense considering the vast amount of real-life movie data the models can utilize to learn; however, they struggle to generate cartoon-level or common-type game asset movies. Even with what they can generate now, the majority include a high level of AI hallucinations (incorrect or misleading results that AI models generate) and very short renditions (3-10 seconds for most), which mostly trigger uncanny valley effects.

There is some excitement for tools like OpenAI's Sora and Google's VideoFX (Veo), and it is likely that this type of tool will have some application in video game cinematics. However, both are still in development and not accessible to the public at the moment. OpenAI's research shows we should expect some issues when those tools are released to the general public. They may misrepresent the physics and properties of

[63] 10 Enterprise license months

[64] How Much Does It Cost To Make A Cinematic Trailer?, Animost Team, https://animost.com/uncategorized/how-much-does-it-cost-to-make-a-cinematic-trailer/,8 November 2023

[65] 3D Animation Costs in 2024: Rates and Budget Management Tips, Rocket Brush Studio, https://rocketbrush.com/blog/how-much-does-3d-animation-cost-per-minute-in-2024-rates-and-budget-management-tips, 27 March 2024

items, cause entities to suddenly appear or disappear, and struggle to simulate interactions between some objects and characters. These issues may limit their use in game cinematics for now. According to OpenAI's research, Sora's quality of output increases proportionally to the computational capabilities of their diffusion models and transformers. Essentially, the more diffusion steps and computer capacity they throw at the problem, the better the output. Sora's algorithms and capabilities are improving continuously, so it's only a question of time before these tools can be leveraged for pre-rendered game cinematics.[66,67]

Base compute 4x compute 32x compute

Regarding real-time rendered movies, the work would require environment building and character animation, assuming some reuse of pre-existing assets. If that is the case, the use of previously demonstrated AI tools for both 3D and 2D renditions would apply.

> *"The first phase of AI helps us improve existing workflows. It might support different parts of the pitch process, for example. But the second phase is more disruptive. A designer with an idea for a character can now generate a video showing that character in-game. If the team likes it, they move forward and build it. The creative process itself is starting to change."*
>
> —Interview with Stephen Peacock
> Director AI at 2K, Ex-Head of AI at AWS & Keywords

For 3D real-time in-game rendered cinematics, utilizing pre-existing models, assuming mostly pre-generated assets, and focusing on animation, would result in a 43% cost efficiency and a corresponding productivity gain of 75%.

---

[66] Video generation models as world simulators, OpenAI, https://openai.com/index/video-generation-models-as-world-simulators/, 15 February 2024
[67] VideoFX, Google's AI Test Kitchen, https://aitestkitchen.withgoogle.com/tools/video-fx, visited August 2024

3D Real-time Rendered (Mid-Range)		Human-only cost	AI-supplemented cost
Environment	Environment design	$1,000	$200
	Superposition & lighting	$2,000	$2,000
Characters	3D Character design	$1,000	$200
	Rigging	$500	$250
	Animation	$8,000	$4,000
	Revisions & Other costs	$1,000	$1,000
AI/Tool cost		$0	$60
Total per minute		**$13,500**	**$7,710**
Cost efficiency			**-42.89%**

3D Real-time Rendered (Mid-Range)	Human-only output	AI-supplemented output
Output	1	1.7510
Productivity gains		**75.10%**

For 2D real-time in-game rendered cinematics, using the pre-existing models, and assuming mostly pre-generated assets, that most of the required work is around animation, and that those animations wouldn't be too complex or different from what is already used and built in-game, would generate a cost efficiency of up to 62% and an according productivity gain of 164%.

2D Real-time Rendered (Mid-Range)		Human-only cost	AI-supplemented cost
Environment	Environment design	$200	$40
	Superposition & lighting	$50	$50
Characters	2D Character design	$200	$40
	Rigging & Animation	$600	$120
	Revisions & Other costs	$200	$200
AI/Tool cost		$0	$24
Total per minute		**$1,250**	**$474**
Cost efficiency			**-62.08%**

2D Real-time Rendered (Mid-Range)	Human-only output	AI-supplemented output
Output	1	2.6371
Productivity gains		**163.71%**

Both of these cases are for real-time rendering only and, as such, could be debated as a best-case scenario. However, note that these techniques can also be used to create pre-rendered movies in various video, game, and 3D engines. There has also been a growing trend to use real-time in-game cutscenes, as game image and rendering quality in game engines have been steadily increasing. As such, the need for prerendering is diminishing. Industry experts estimate that real-time renditions now cover 70-80% of cinematics, and this number is expected to continue growing steadily. [68]

Per the above, there's been a trend for pre-rendered movies to disappear from the market gradually, but as Sora and other similar tools' capabilities improve, and production costs of this process diminish, we may see the trend turn around, and pre-rendered movies' popularity could come back over the next few years.

"At OpenAI, one of the Sora evangelists showed us a three or four minute video of a game concept. It looked like finished AAA gameplay. He built the whole thing in three days. The video included character design, game flow, mechanics, and sound. It was a complete, compelling pitch that replaced weeks or months of traditional work."

—Interview with Stephen Peacock
Director AI at 2K, Ex-Head of AI at AWS & Keywords

"C'est toujours dans la productivité que ça se passe. Je pense que les jouets (IA) qui existent aujourd'hui vont donner place à de l'innovation. [...] Comme les vidéos GenAI, pour moi, il y a une technologie là-dedans qui est vraiment intéressante. Je pense qu'on a les bases là-dedans du rendering du futur."

AI translation: "It's always about productivity. I think the (AI) toys that exist today will give way to innovation. [...] Like the GenAI videos, for me, there's a technology in there that's really interesting. I think we have the basis for the rendering of the future."

—Interview with Pierre-Paul Giroux
Vice-President Engineering A.I. at Unity

---

[68] How Video Is Failing To Enhance And Promote Games, Barry Jenkins, Forbes, https://www.forbes.com/councils/forbestechcouncil/2021/09/17/how-video-is-failing-to-enhance-and-promote-games/, 17 September 2021

6.4 AUDIO CREATION

Game audio is vital to video game development, contributing to a game's immersive experience. It is essential for expressing feelings and strengthening the story. Game audio creation requires both artistic and technical skills. Audio pros must work closely with game designers, programmers, and other artists to create a unified experience. A game has three main audio elements: sound effects (SFX), music, and, if present, voiceovers.

Artificial Intelligence is playing an increasingly important role in game audio creation, revolutionizing the development and implementation of sound effects, music, and voiceovers. It can generate sound effects on the fly, speed up sound and music prototyping, generate soundtracks that match the game's narrative, and ease post-production editing by automating mixing and mastering.

Audio typically accounts for 5-10% of a game development budget, as outlined in the breakdown below. The actual split can vary depending on the game and audio design choices, as well as whether audio is an integral part of the gameplay.

Game audio budget	Low %	High %
Sound Effects (SFX)	30%	40%
Music	30%	40%
Voiceovers (VO)	25%	35%

Below is a typical allocation built on a 7% audio budget allocation for a $10 million project.

Game audio budget	%	$
Sound Effects (SFX)	35.7%	$250,000
Music	35.7%	$250,000
Voiceovers (VO)	28.6%	$200,000
Total	**100%**	**$700,000**

According to this budget and the analyses explained in the following subsections, we can extrapolate an 86% cost-effectiveness of using AI in audio creation pipelines, along with a corresponding 597% productivity gain. An almost 7-fold output increase for the same cost.

High end AA – Audio cost	Human-only cost	AI-supplemented cost		Variation
		Human	AI	
Sound Effects (SFX)	$250,000	$50,000	$1,320	-79.47%
Music	$250,000	$25,000	$120	-89.95%
Voiceovers (VO)	$200,000	$20,000	$3,960	-88.02%
Total	**$700,000**	**$95,000**	**$5,400**	**-85.66%**
Total	**$700,000**	**$100,400**		**-85.66%**
Total %	**100.00%**	**13.57%**	**0.77%**	**-85.66%**

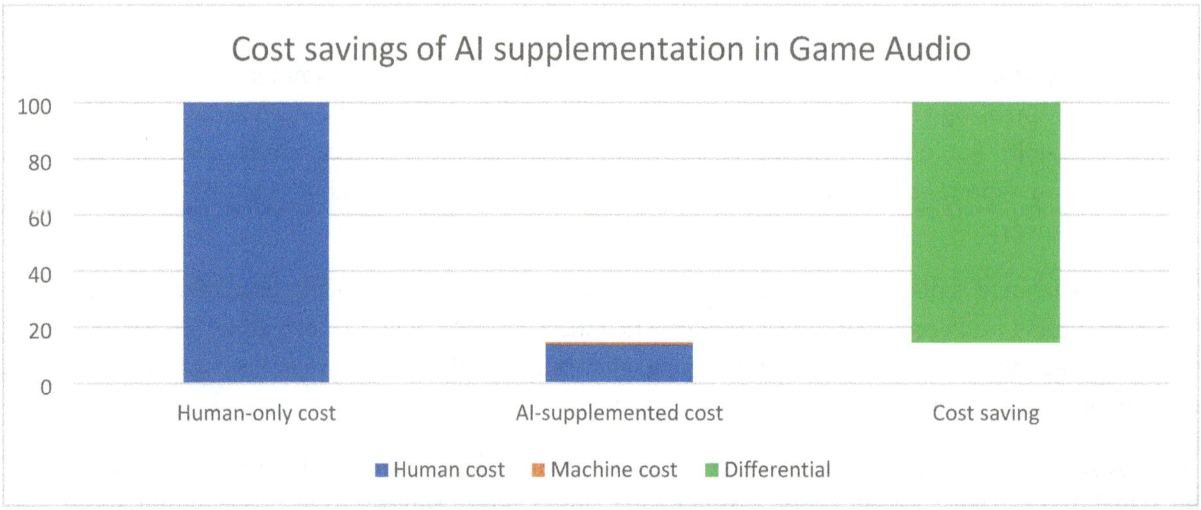

High end AA – Audio output	Human Design	AI-supported Design
Output	1	6.9721
Productivity gains		597.21%

High end AA – Audio output	Human-only Human cost & output	AI-supplemented Human cost & output	AI-supplemented Machine cost	AI-supplemented Machine output
Value 1	$700,000	$95,000	$5,400	$605,000
Ratio 1	100.00%	13.57%	0.77%	86.43%
Ratio AI-sup	697.21%	**94.62%**	5.38%	**602.59%**

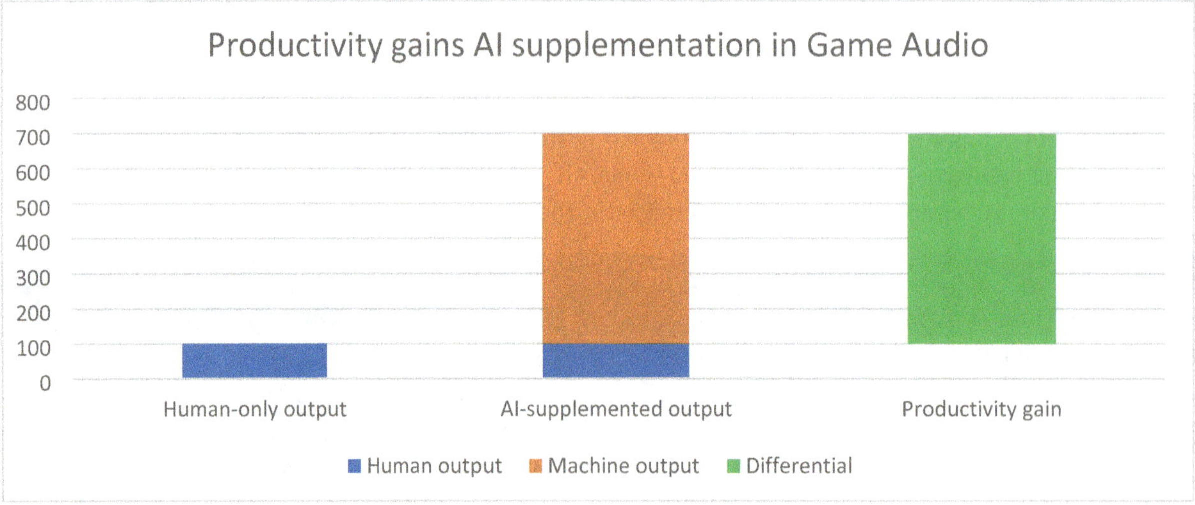

6.4.1 Sound effects

Sound effects are the audio cues accompanying in-game actions and events. They range from footsteps and weapon sounds to ambient noises. Well-designed SFX can significantly improve the player's immersion and provide important gameplay feedback.

SFX creators can charge between $10 and $200 per sound effect, with most charging $300 to $500 per minute of game ambiance sounds.[69,70]

Sound Effects Tier	Pricing per SFX
Low-end	$10-40
Mid-tier	$40-75
High-end	$75-200

A typical sound effects project for a game can cost between $500 and $100,000. Costs vary depending on the project's complexity, length, and urgency, as well as the legal licensing terms associated with its audio assets. Rates shown above assume a full ownership license. A license to use these assets without owning them would cost approximately 50% of what is presented here. An average SFX project for a high-end AA game of $10,000,000 will cost approximately $250,000, or 2.5% of the full game budget.

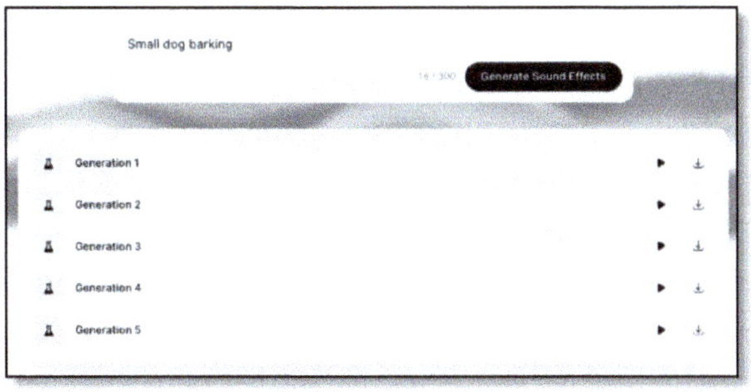

There is a growing number of available tools to generate SFX. One of the most popular tools is ElevenLabs' Text-to-Sound. It can generate multiple, downloadable, fully licensed sound effects from simple text prompts in seconds. For game SFX, the best AI matches most human-made work. It can replace 70-90% of human-only sound effects, depending on the required quality and complexity. For the sake of conservative research, we'll build this analysis on a 70% value. The cost of ElevenLabs subscriptions for commercial use starts as low as $5 per month for 750 seconds of Text-to-Sound effect, and up to $1,320 per month for 275,000 seconds of Text-to-Sound effect. Assuming a 4-second average per sound effect, generation cost varies between ≈$0.02 and $0.035 per sound effect.[71]

Plan	Monthly cost	SFX seconds	# SFX (4sec)	$ per sec	$ per SFX
Starter	5	750	187	0.006667	0.026667
Creator	22	2,500	625	0.0088	0.0352
Pro	99	12,500	3,125	0.00792	0.03168
Scale	330	50,000	12,500	0.0066	0.0264
Business	1320	275,000	68,750	0.0048	0.0192
Enterprise	Custom	Custom	Custom	Custom	Custom

Even by choosing the most conservative savings projection and 4 months of a Scale-level license to span an average high-level SFX project length, we can achieve a 69% cost efficiency and 228% productivity gain.

[69] How much do video game sound effects cost? A comprehensive guide, ElevenLabs, https://elevenlabs.io/blog/how-much-do-video-game-sound-effects-cost, 9 April 2024
[70] Budget for sound design in video games, Mikhail Repin, https://repinsound.com/tpost/9o29zahie1-budget-for-sound-design-in-video-games, 4 May 2023
[71] How to incorporate AI sound effect generators in your game development process, ElevenLabs, https://elevenlabs.io/blog/ai-sound-effect-generators-in-games, 10 April 2024

When looking at the most efficient pipelines, we could achieve 89% cost efficiency and 850% productivity gain. Average impact potential would be 79% cost efficiency and 387% productivity gain.

SFX	Human-only cost	AI Low End	AI Average	AI High End
Human cost	$250,000	$75,000	$50,000	$25,000
AI/Tool cost	$0	$1,320	$1,320	$1,320
Total	**$250,000**	**$76,320**	**$51,320**	**$26,320**
Cost efficiency		-69.47%	-79.47%	-89.47%

SFX	Human-only output	AI Low End	AI Average	AI High End
Output	1	3.2757	4.8714	9.4985
Productivity gains		**227.57%**	**387.14%**	**849.85%**

Notably, feedback from interviews suggests that current levels of AI SFX are meeting and exceeding the quality and utility of SFX asset libraries. Meaning that although SFX asset libraries are competitively priced, AI SFX generation is starting to become more cost-efficient than what is currently widely used in the market in some cases, especially when it comes to the purchase and use of fully licensed owned audio. It also means, though, that a team that's already extensively using externally purchased assets instead of creating them internally from scratch may find minimal cost efficiencies and productivity gains, in contrast to what is shown above.

6.4.2 Music

Game music sets the emotional tone and atmosphere of the game. It can be dynamic, adapting to the player's actions and game states, or static, providing a consistent backdrop to gameplay. Music composers work to create themes and scores to help players connect to the game world.

The cost of producing game music can vary between $50 and $2,500 per minute of music, depending on the professional level of the hired artists and editing team, as well as the type of license related to the created or purchased assets. An average game music project for a high-end AA game of $10,000,000 will cost about $250,000, or 2.5% of a full game budget. At a high mid-tier $1,000 per music minute, that would mean 250 minutes (4hr 10min) worth of usable and licensable music for a game. [72,73]

Music Tier	Pricing per music minute
Low-end	$50-300
Mid-tier	$300-1,200
High-end	$1,200-2,500

[72] Understanding how much a game music project costs, Flutu, https://flutumusic.com/understanding-how-much-a-game-music-project-costs/, visited September 2024

[73] Budgeting for Audio in Your Game's Crowdfunding Campaign, Kole Hicks, Game Developer, https://www.gamedeveloper.com/audio/budgeting-for-audio-in-your-game-s-crowdfunding-campaign, 23 May 2016

"If you're new to music creation and want to turn a poem into a song, the AI might generate decent lyrics and a basic backing track. That's enough to make something you're proud to share with friends or family. But if you're a professional songwriter, the tool needs to offer much more control before it's truly useful."

—Interview with Stephen Peacock
Director AI at 2K, Ex-Head of AI at AWS & Keywords

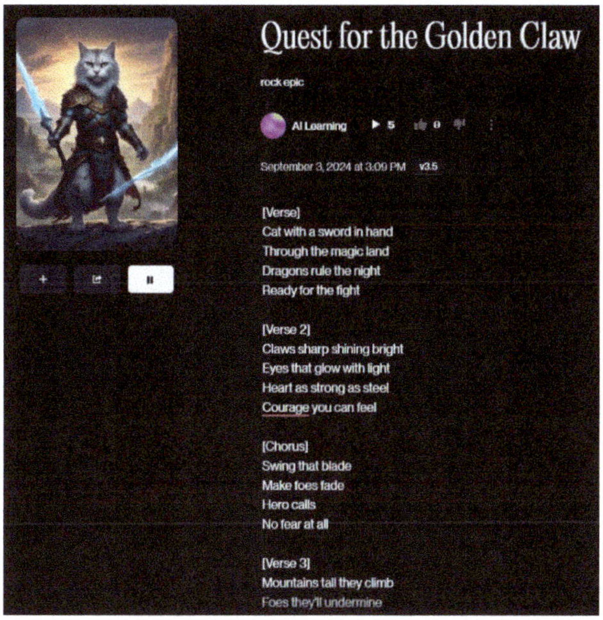

Over the last year, developers have released and updated multiple AI music tools, such as Stability's AI Stable Audio and Google's MusicFX, but Udio and Suno are currently the two most notable and popular ones.

We self-experimented with Suno v3.5 and researched self-reported user feedback. With self-use, we were able to generate, on the first prompt, 2 professional-level songs, with the same lyrics and slightly different styles within a few seconds. The output contained generated verses, chorus, pre-chorus, final chorus, bridge, instrumental solos, interludes, etc. Twelve outputs generated through different prompts were all of professional or semi-professional quality, which surpasses 95%+ of music currently used in the game industry.[74]

Standard non-AI production that does exceed Suno's quality is usually quite expensive and falls in the high-end tier, and even then, may have some difficulty meeting the bar of a professional music prompter who can tweak and adapt their ask to get what they need within a few prompts. Most game developers could use generated Suno outputs directly, or make minimal changes before game implementation. Considering this, we assume this could easily reduce music generation efforts by ≈90% for game purposes. We believe that the actual number is greater than this, approaching 99%, particularly for instrumental (non-vocal) songs, and that it will continue to increase as generative models improve. However, we want to maintain a conservative value to manage bias. Here is an example of Suno use.

Prompt: A videogame rock song about a sword-wielding cat fighting a dragon

Output 1 : https://suno.com/song/a4638dc8-1d94-4a1b-bd46-8b8291c282f2

Output 2 : https://suno.com/song/8a0931b4-38a2-4fa9-9ab7-bf0652125e63

---

[74] Suno, https://suno.com/, visited September 2024

Suno offers 3 plans, 2 of which include fully licensable commercial use of created songs. It can also offer customizable enterprise agreements for larger needs. On the platform, every song generation costs 5 credits. The way their paid plans work is that once you've run out of monthly credits, you can still enjoy the same benefits as free users and can generate up to 10 songs (50 credits) daily until the monthly credits renew. Music creators are self-reporting that to achieve a desirable outcome, they must spend between 10 and 150 credits per song (2 to 30 generations) for song extensions and remixing. The average cost across creators is 54 credits (almost 11 generations). Even without utilizing the daily extension's full potential, and assuming you need 54 credits to produce a usable song instead of the platform-reported 5, the practical cost of using this platform ranges from $0.16 to $0.22 per generated song.

Suno	Commercial use	Price	Credits	Songs (54c)	Price/Song (54c)
Basic	No	$0	50/day	0.9	$0.00
Pro	Yes	$10/month	2,500/month*	46.3	$0.22
Premier	Yes	$30/month	10,000/month*	185.2	$0.16
Custom	Yes	Custom	Custom	Custom	Custom

*+10/day when monthly allocations run out.

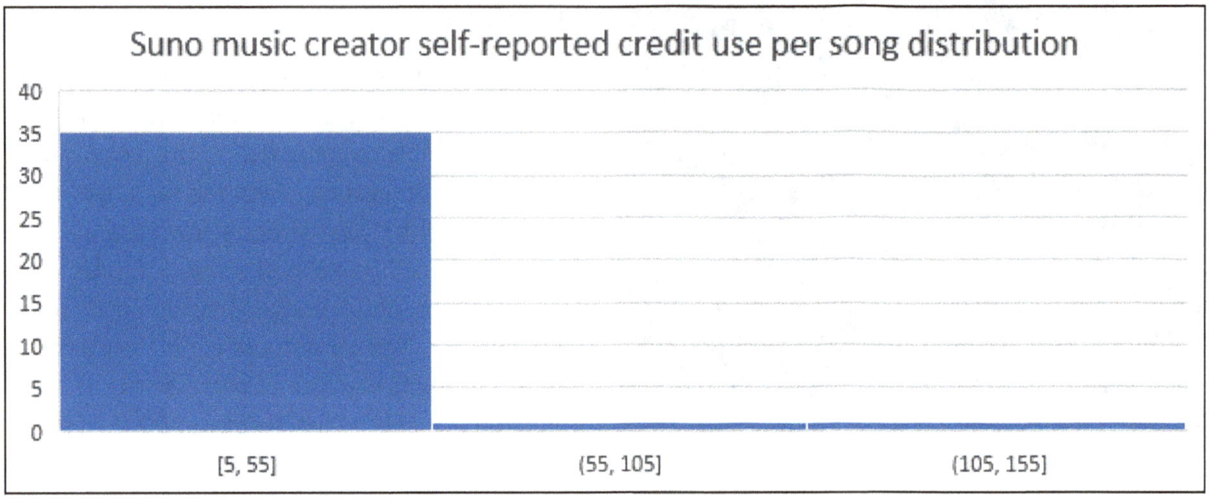

"I see in my mind, a game like Assassin's Creed 75, and another like Stardew Valley or Undertale. For a game like Assassin's Creed 75, using GenAI music would definitely be fine. It's consumable media. [...] But I don't thing that AI music is would work with games that people have a real emotional connection to, like Stardew Valley or Undertale. Especially when someone sounds excited when they're talking about a game, I think this one you can't replace. [...] You can create definitely high quality content that people enjoy consuming. Which isn't bad, it's just a different product."

—Interview with Dylan Ebert, PhD
Developer Advocate Engineer, Hugging Face

We self-experimented with Udio-130 & Udio-32 v1.5 models and researched self-reported user feedback. While the models seem to be able to generate more customized content than Suno, and the audio sounds cleaner and clearer, users report that the tool is less user-friendly and less consistent in terms of output. This makes its use a bit more challenging for music neophytes and potentially better suited for current music professionals than the general public. Output length capabilities are also less than Suno at the moment (2m10s and 32s long songs for Udio-130 & Udio-32 vs. 4m for Suno), and thus often require song extensions. These Udio song extensions also have consistency issues within the same song. They often require more effort, both on and off the platform, before they are ready to use. The tool requires more time, effort, and precise prompting than Suno's to generate the desired outputs. It remains an impressive tool and could automate approximately 60% of human-only music generation processes for gaming purposes, especially with the new Udio-130 model. [75]

Prompt: A videogame rock song about a sword-wielding cat fighting a dragon, hard rock, epic rock, heavy metal

Output 1 : https://www.udio.com/songs/3sqykvEhJtmFA8wd7Zv3PW

Output 2: https://www.udio.com/songs/1YdiJ6Nv1BdUYuy5BTikpz

[75] Udio beta, https://www.udio.com/, visited September 2024

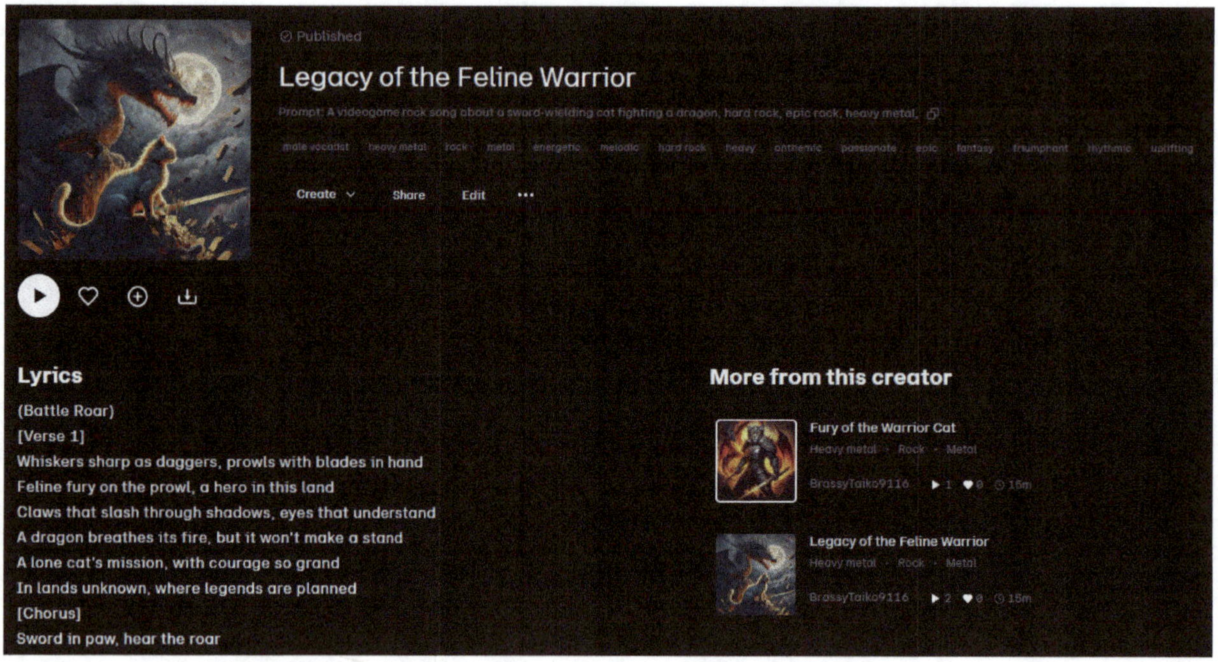

Udio offers three monthly pricing plans, all of which provide full licensable commercial use of created songs. The free plan requires users to provide attribution to Udio for any created content that is redistributed and/or used commercially. Music creators report needing to spend between 6 and 300 credits per song for song extensions and remixes. The average spend is 97 credits per song. Assuming you need 97 credits to obtain a usable song, rather than the platform-reported 5 or 6, the cost of using this platform is $0.61 to $0.81 per generated song. This cost calculation is based on the monthly subscription plans shown below. Extra credit plans would cost more, between $2.43 and $2.91 per song.

Udio	Commercial use	Price	Credits	Songs (97c)	Price/Song
Free	With attribution	$0	100/month	1.0	$0.00
Standard	Yes	$10/month	1,200/month	12.4	$0.81
Pro	Yes	$30/month	4,800/month	49.5	$0.61
Extra	Yes*	$3	100	1.0	$2.91
Extra	Yes*	$25	1,000	10.3	$2.43

*With Udio credit attribution if no subscription plans are active.

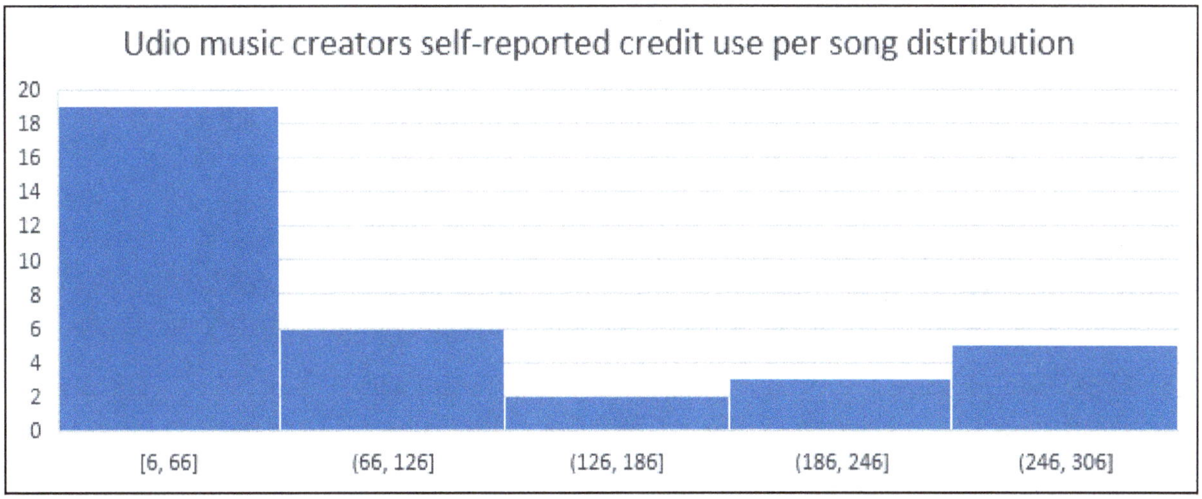

By applying four months of the most expensive licenses to a project, we can achieve cost efficiencies of 90% and 60%, along with productivity gains of nearly 900% and 150% for Suno and Udio use, respectively. The low cost of the license relative to human salaries means that its impact on calculation is minimal (0.05% cost on a $250,000 music project budget).

Music creation	Human-only cost	Suno-supported cost	Udio-supported cost
Human cost	$250,000	$25,000	$100,000
AI/Tool cost	$0	$120	$120
Total	**$250,000**	$25,120	$100,120
Cost efficiency		**-89.95%**	**-59.95%**

Music creation	Human-only output	Suno-supported output	Udio-supported output
Output	1	9.9522	2.4970
Productivity gains		**895.22%**	**149.70%**

"I don't use it for music. I think music is the soul of the game. So I really like to make my own music for it."

—Interview with Dylan Ebert, PhD
Developer Advocate Engineer, Hugging Face

6.4.3 Voiceovers

Voice actors bring characters to life by delivering dialogue, narration, and other vocal performances. High-quality voiceovers (VOs) can significantly improve game storytelling and character development. This process involves casting, studio logistics, directing, recording voice actors, and implementing the recorded dialogue into the game.

> *"Pronunciation is a speech element that is complicated to manage: while it is performed "naturally" by human, AI requires a proper speech technology and specific features so to fully control it and manage it efficiently."*
>
> —Interview with Andrea Ballista
> Founder & CEO, Voiseed

The cost of producing game voiceovers can vary greatly if present as a game design choice. A typical game voiceover character costs between $2,500 and $5,000 for 2 days of actor recording and related post-production, with low-end budgets falling below that mark and high-end budget teams formed of highly recognized and experienced professionals exceeding that. These costs include actor casting, studio leasing, audio engineers, sound designers, and producers.[76,77,78]

Game voiceover budget	Low-end %	High-end %
Voice actor fee	55%	60%
Studio time	15%	20%
Audio engineer	10%	15%
Voice direction	10%	15%

> *"In dealing with AI Voices solutions, it is important to consider "content tiering" (from narrative content to very expressive content): not all the type of content can be perfectly managed with a "full synthetic approach". In dealing with complex interpretations, that crafts the emotional feeling of a character, the human voice actors are surely the best solutions."*
>
> —Interview with Andrea Ballista
> Founder & CEO, Voiseed

An average game VO project for a high-end AA game of $10,000,000 will cost about $200,000, or 2% of the full game budget. At a high mid-tier $5,000 per character, that would mean about 40 characters' worth of usable and licensable VO for a game, or 80 days' worth of VO audio recording. Most professional voice actors can work for about 4-6 hours per day in the recording booth, with an average of 5 hours per day.

---

[76] How much do video game sound effects cost?: How much do video game voiceovers cost?, ElevenLabs, https://elevenlabs.io/blog/how-much-do-video-game-sound-effects-cost, 9 April 2024

[77] What to Charge as a Voiceover Artist, Backstage, https://www.backstage.com/magazine/article/voiceover-artist-rate-guide-834/, 22 February 2024

[78] A VO's Journey Voice Over Rate Guide, Anthony Pica, https://www.avosjourney.com/voice-over-rate-guide, visited September 2024

For complex work, such as character voices, every hour of recording yields an output of 10-15 minutes of finished and usable content, averaging 12.5 minutes. In this scenario, the output would be 5,000 minutes of character voiceovers.

(80 VO days) x (5h recording / VO day) x (12.5 minutes of VO / h recording) = 5,000 minutes of VO

$200,000 / 5,000 minutes of VO = $40 / minute of VO

VO Tier	Average cost per character (2 days of recording)	Cost per game character VO output minute (average)
Indie (Low-Tier)	$0-2,500$	$0-20
Non-Union rates (Mid-Tier)	$2,500-5,000$	$20-40
Union rates (High-Tier)	$5,000+	$40+

There is a growing number of available tools to generate AI VOs, and a growing number of business cases of videogame organizations using such tools for their games' VOs. The most popular and versatile ones at the moment are ElevenLabs'. ElevenLabs' Text-to-Speech and Voice Changer (Speech-to-Speech and Voice Cloning) tools can generate ready-to-use and near-ready-to-use fully licensed voice recordings. The platform requires either source text or source voice recordings, along with the stylistic choices for the destination speech, which can be selected through their platform.[79,80,81]

"The type of tools we offer were not used at all before. I think that clients will first focus on localizing their back catalogues, but will then soon start using it as their main tool, even in original languages ."

—Interview with Tim Lupo
Co-founder & CEO of Deeptune, Forbes 30 Under 30 2024

For games' VO creation, ElevenLabs' best Text-to-Speech generations match most human-generated work. It can replace about 50% to 70% of human VOs, depending on the desired quality and complexity. The tool's limitation is usually related to its restricted capabilities for fluctuations and variations in emotional tone. The platform lacks a clear way to convey emotions, relying solely on punctuation or contextual text cues, if understood at all. Therefore, the tools still struggle to express emotions effectively.

[79] Paradox Interactive speeds up audio generation from weeks to hours with ElevenLabs, ElevenLabs, https://elevenlabs.io/blog/paradox-interactive, 30 June 2023
[80] Creating realistic AI generated character voices for games, ElevenLabs, https://elevenlabs.io/blog/ai-generated-character-voices-for-games, 21 June 2024
[81] AMGI and ElevenLabs partnership, AMGI Studios, https://x.com/amgistudios/status/1811786492542415318, 12 July 2024

"If you have a technology and process that enables to generate completely voice a script from scratch, then you do not need localization as we've known it. Then we can generate the other languages applying the same emotional map applied on the source script to regenerate the machine translated script lines, even preserving the same casting choices. This is basically changing everything, there is no more the need of a voice recording studio: you just need to have the ability to "generated and select the best generated takes to be included in the game", a kind of "AI Voice Director"."

—Interview with Andrea Ballista
Founder & CEO, Voiseed

ElevenLabs' Voice Changer (Speech-to-Speech) tool has a greater matching capability regarding pronunciation, intonation, and emotion conveying than Text-to-Speech, as it emulates directly a source-voiced sound file into a newly generated voice file. The quality can replace 90%+ of human-only VO for games. But it needs a source audio voice recording to be generated and fed to the platform. The effort is approximately 80% of a human-only process due to the addition of this new step. In the case of voice cloning, the platform would also require you to provide at least 30 minutes of audio, with 3 hours being the optimal amount of time needed as a source.

"The main value proposition of our AI tool is that it makes production cheaper. [...] On our platform, it costs about $1 a minute to dub."

—Interview with Tim Lupo
Co-founder & CEO of Deeptune, Forbes 30 Under 30 2024

The cost of ElevenLabs commercial-use subscriptions starts as low as $5 per month for 30 Text-to-Speech/Speech-to-Speech minutes, and up to $1,320 per month for 11,000 minutes of the same. The platform also now offers up to 2 free regenerations, which reduces the need to spend more than 1 generation per VO string if needed, and lowers the actual cost per VO minute.

Plan	Monthly cost	VO minutes	$ per VO minute
Starter	$5	30	$0.167
Creator	$22	100	$0.22
Pro	$99	500	$0.198
Scale	$330	2,000	$0.165
Business	$1,320	11,000	$0.12
Enterprise	Custom	Custom	Custom

To be conservative, we will base our analysis on a 3-month business license (or 12 months of a scale license). This would easily cover our precalculated scenario of 5,000 minutes. It would also allow for regeneration, revision, rework, or schedule changes as needed. We'll also be using a 60% average work efficiency gain for ElevenLabs Text-to-Speech capabilities and 80% for its Speech-to-Speech capabilities.

> *"The tool can also change the way developer can build the game. The tech allows a very cheap and fast generation of expressive voice placeholder, which reduce cost, accelerate gameplay and QA testing sooner, faster bug fixing, increased game quality and faster market releases."*
>
> —Interview with Andrea Ballista
> Founder & CEO, Voiseed

Based on the calculations and assumptions made above, the most conservative outlooks yield a 58% cost efficiency and a 138% productivity gain. When examining the most efficient pipelines with Speech-to-Speech, we achieve 88% cost efficiency and a 735% productivity gain.

VOs	Human-only cost	Text-to-Speech supplemented cost	Speech-to-Speech supplemented cost
Human cost	$200,000	$80,000	$20,000
AI/Tool cost	$0	$3,960	$3,960
Total	**$200,000**	**$83,960**	**$23,960**
Cost efficiency		**-58.02%**	**-88.02%**

VOs	Human-only output	Text-to-Speech supplemented output	Speech-to-Speech supplemented output
Output	1	2.3821	8.3472
Productivity gains		**138.21%**	**734.72%**

"AI dubbing is not yet as good as human dubbing. But there's going to be a moment, probably in 2025, where AI dubbing is objectively better to watch, as the quality increases. And it'll be 10 times faster and maybe 100 times cheaper, which I think will rapidly encourage people to transform their dubbing businesses, from these voice actor driven businesses, to more editor-style driven businesses. Where they only have an editor in the loop using software like ours."

—Interview with Tim Lupo
Co-founder & CEO of Deeptune, Forbes 30 Under 30 2024

"Considering quality level expectation for indie games, some of them may just decide to use 100% AI voices. Even if may be not "perfect", it may open-up 30+ new market. There are also a lot of AA games that have similar need, so they can use the AI voices for NPC and secondary characters, integrating voice production with some real voice actors for major characters. While for indie developers there will be significant saving around 80-90% external voice recording cost (you still need to have "AI voice specialist" support for each of the published languages), for AA production it really depends on the nature of the game and from the humans/virtual casting ratio, but we can expect something between 40 and 60% savings."

—Interview with Andrea Ballista
Founder & CEO, Voiseed

6.5 QUALITY ASSURANCE

Game testing, commonly called quality assurance (QA) testing, refers to playing prototypes of video games to identify errors, known as bugs, in the game industry. Game testers typically work closely with game development engineers and other technical team members. They provide feedback and bug reports to game developers so they can fix game errors prior to public release.

> *"AI game testing can easily automate 50% of the necessary manual effort."*
>
> —Interview with Matt Ditton
> CEO and Co-Founder of Mighty Games Group & Mighty Build and Test

The following is an AI QA automation support business case. It was built by a QA service provider for an application to a AAA MMO Unreal-engine shooter. The team analyzed the potential cost reductions achievable through AI QA use. They've applied their calculations to a previously human-only executed project, enabling them to compare human-only and AI-assisted QA performance accurately. Below are their results, where:

- Test Type: represents the type of QA testing applied to the game.
- Manual QA hours: is the amount of monthly manual effort needed to complete the test.
- AI/Auto QA coverage: is the ratio of manual work that the AI tools would automate.
- Saved QA hours: is the monthly manual work hours reduced by AI automation.
- Remaining QA hours: is the amount of human manual work hours left to do after AI automation.

Test Types & Monthly hours	Manual QA hours	AI/Auto QA coverage	Saved QA hours	Remaining QA hours
Boot Check	32	100%	-32	0
Build Verification Testing	640	80%	-512	128
Exploratory Testing	640	0%	0	640
Functional Testing	1024	20%	-204.8	819.2
Network / Multiplayer Testing	512	80%	-409.6	102.4
Regression Testing	256	70%	-179.2	76.8
User Experience Testing	160	0%	0	160
Accessibility Testing	160	0%	0	160
Platform Integration	128	50%	-64	64
Certification Testing	400	50%	-200	200
Performance Testing	512	70%	-358.4	153.6
Compatibility Testing	200	100%	-200	0
Load & Soak Testing	200	100%	-200	0
Recovery Testing	128	90%	-115.2	12.8
Localization Testing (LQA)	640	70%	-448	192
Totals	**5632**		**-2923.2**	**2708.8**

Some very basic or repetitive tasks could be fully, or almost fully, automated. This is the case for "boot checks" (making sure that a game build can start properly) or compatibility testing (verifying base performance and functionality across different platforms or types of computers).

> *"If we assume that the scope of work stays the same, using our AI tool reduces the time spent on tasks by 25 to 80%, depending on the game's complexity, emergence, and required length of reasoning steps."*
>
> —Interview with Christoffer Holmgård
> CEO and Co-Founder of modl.ai

More complex tasks, specifically those requiring the subjective point of view or extensive experience from testers, cannot be automated at all using AI. That's the case for exploratory testing, and especially for one of its subtypes, destructive testing. It often requires vast experience and proper instinct from testers to deduce where a game developer would likely have omitted a functionality, thus breaking the initially expected outcome of a game feature. Essentially, reading a game creator's mind to "feel" where there's likely going to be a bug, and then exploiting it.

> *"Classic QA work organizations have been surprisingly ill-suited to driving QA with AI agents. I think it has to do with the fact that most QA work really exploits human intelligence to the max. There's vagueness in descriptions, an assumption that a user will simply pick-up on any issues seen. One learning for me has been how alien automation is, to human-like behavior."*
>
> —Interview with Christoffer Holmgård
> CEO and Co-Founder of modl.ai

It's also true for user experience (UX) and accessibility (A11Y) testing. They require a real person, sometimes with specific disabilities, to play the game and provide feedback on what they like or dislike about the game, or what they can or cannot do as a target end user.

"I think there's other applications from a dev perspective, definitely on the automation side of things in build processes. Not only on continuous integration and looking for build errors, identifying who submitted that code that doesn't compile properly and broke the build, but also automatically fixing that. And tying very much with automated tests and unit testing, as well as soak testing, smoke testing, and all of the kinds of playtesting."

—Interview with Jamie Campbell
Founder of MTX Solutions, Co-Founder of d3t Studio, ex-ATI (AMD), ex-Technical Director at THQ

Following this evaluation, the AI QA team projected significant efficiency gains and/or cost reductions in various types of quality assurance testing. The team could automate more than half of the planned human-only manual QA work with AI agents. When considering the cost of AI implementation, integrating AI agents into the development pipeline would result in a 24.75% cost efficiency and a corresponding 32.9% productivity gain.

QA costs	Cost	% Of Original Monthly Spend
Human-only	$190,912.00	100.00%
Human AI-supplemented	$93,654.80	49.06%
Human cost reduction from AI	**-$97,257.20**	**-50.94%**
AI QA tool cost	+$50,000	+26.19%
Total spend	**$143,654.80**	**75.25%**
Total cost savings	**-$47,257.20**	**-24.75%**

QA	Human-only cost	AI-supplemented cost		Variation
		Human	AI	
Quality Assurance Testing	$190,912.00	$93,654.80	$50,000.00	-24.75%
Total	**$190,912.00**	**$143,654.80**		**-24.75%**
Total %	**100.00%**	**49.06%**	**26.19%**	**-24.75%**

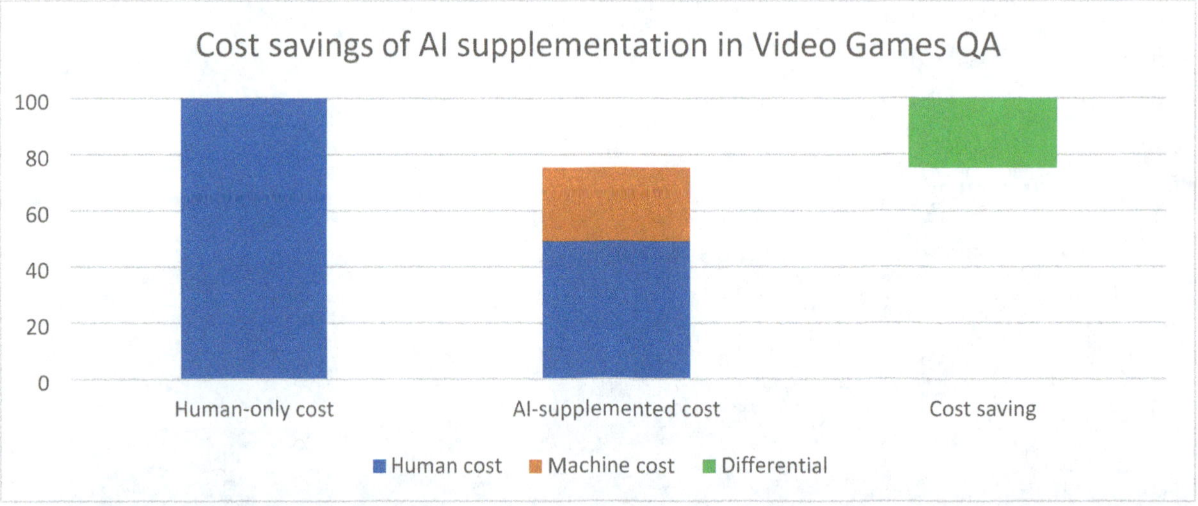

QA	Human-only output	AI-supplemented output
Output	1	1.3290
Productivity gains		**32.90%**

QA output	Human-only Human cost & output	AI-supplemented Human cost & output	AI-supplemented Machine cost	AI-supplemented Machine output
Value 1	$190,912	$93,654.80	$50,000	$97,257.20
Ratio 1	100.00%	49.06%	26.19%	50.94%
Ratio AI-sup	132.90%	**65.19%**	34.81%	**67.70%**

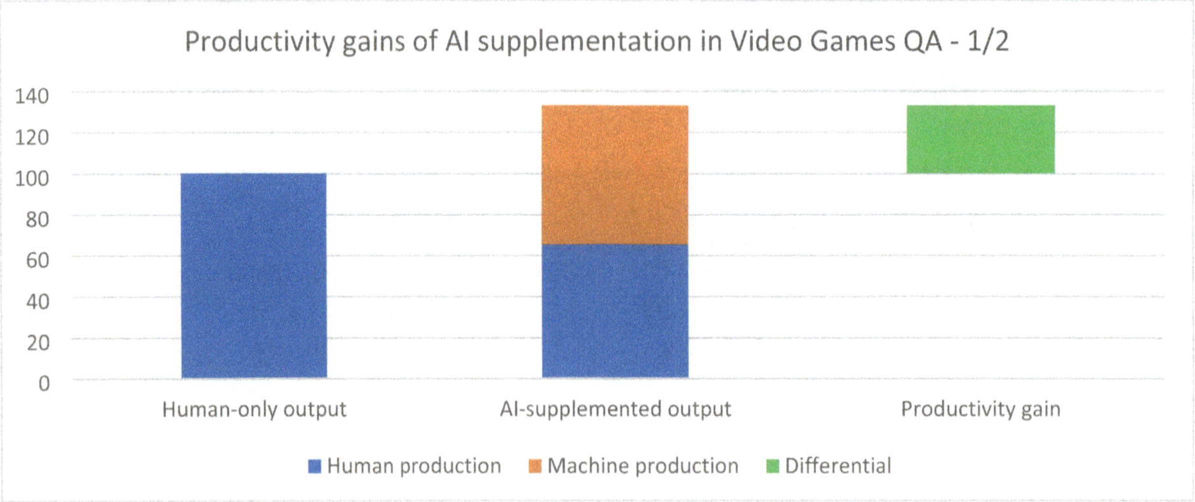

"I think where things could get a lot more efficient is things like bug fixing and the analysis of tying in QA bug reports to identifying where those issues stem from. What's the root cause of that bug in code and can we fix that with Gen AI? Alpha to Gold master, that time is extremely critical. It's incredibly stressful. It's when all teams are crunching. It's got human cost to it as well as financial cost. If you're late getting to that gold master, it's going to cost you significantly in marketing, reputational damage."

—Interview with Jamie Campbell
Founder of MTX Solutions, Co-Founder of d3t Studio, ex-ATI (AMD), ex-Technical Director at THQ

Two caveats to take into consideration here, though, are that output from both manual and automated QA is rarely linear, especially when a high amount of QA work is applied to a project. Output is usually more regressive, similar to a Pareto or cumulative distribution function (CDF).[82]

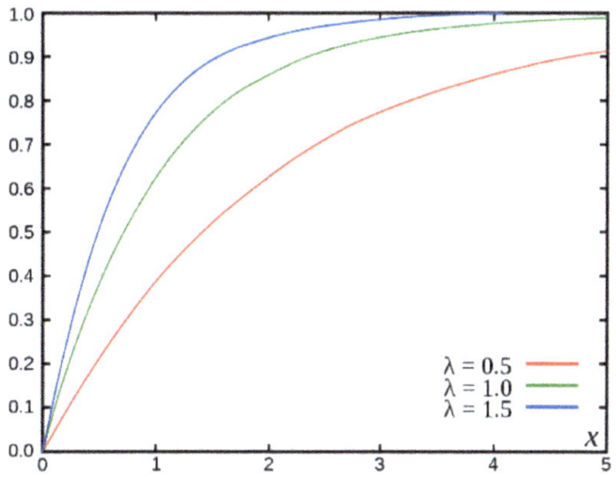

Despite this, though, "live" MMO games, like the one used in the previous analysis, have a high amount of content that is usually tested minimally, or not at all, due to the complexity of the title and, more specifically, the high number of game assets and related test permutation complexities.

"Combinatorics is where it really starts lifting up the productivity. [...] Imagine a game in 15 languages and 30 different devices that needs to be tested on every build. That's a lot of testing, to the extent that it doesn't even get done at the moment because nobody has that many testers."

-Interview with Christoffer Holmgård
CEO and Co-Founder of modl.ai

An example of those permutations could be a live update to a game, adding 20 new hats, 20 new armors, and 20 new weapons to a game that already boasts 100 hats, armors, and weapons.

[82] Cumulative distribution function, Wikipedia, https://en.wikipedia.org/wiki/Cumulative_distribution_function, visited June 2024

Should you test the new content as a standalone exercise, and the related permutations of hats to armors to weapons, you would need to test out 8,000 sets (20 hats x 20 armors x 20 weapons), which is already quite a lot of effort. The reality is that in this scenario, which happens frequently with current live games, you would have to test out the new content against all of the previously existing inventory. Assuming that the team already executed 100% of that work (1,000,000 permutations), they would still need to verify 728,000 new permutations with this new live update.

	Live update	Pre-existing content	New total content
Hats	20	100	120
Armors	20	100	120
Weapons	20	100	120
Permutations	8,000	1,000,000	1,728,000
Diff. Permutations	N/A	0	728,000

Assuming a very conservative amount of time of 1 minute per test for each new permutation, testing only this minor update would require more than 6 human work years to complete.

Minutes	728,000
Hours	12,133.33
Work days (8h per day)	1,516.67
Work years (250 days per year)	6.07

Updates like these are done frequently in live games – quarterly, sometimes monthly, and usually cover more content than just extra items. This is also one of the testing types that automation, and especially AI agents, should cover. Work that no human tester would have done previously, as the human cost would far outpace the return on investment. Considering this, and even when assuming productivity outputs that follow a cumulative distribution (regressive) function, QA coverage and productivity gains could grow drastically with AI agents.

> *"We tend to think of our AI tool as an output enhancer, or an accelerant. I would say that the output it provides is 6x to 16x more than classic methods."*
>
> —Interview with Christoffer Holmgård
> CEO and Co-Founder of modl.ai

If we adapt the previously given scenario, the newly generated output stemming from testing this new content would bring no additional human or AI costs, as no additional human effort is needed, and the new work can simply be tackled by the same AI agents. Assuming a similarly sized update would be released every 2 months, which is quite typical in the industry, the productivity gain from AI QA automation would increase to 176.05%, representing a significant improvement over human-only QA. Note, though, that it would not technically generate a different cost-savings as determined previously, as this is content that would not normally be tested via human-only practices anyway.

Human-only output (hours)	5,632h
Human-only cost ($)	$190,912
Human-only average hourly cost ($/h)	33.90 $/h
2 months drop Human-only cost (h)	12,133.33h
1 month drop Human-only cost (h) equivalent	6,066.67h
1 month drop Human-only cost ($) equivalent	$205,646.21
1 month original Human-only cost ($)	$190,912
1 month new Human-only cost ($) equivalent	$396,558.21

QA	Human-only cost	AI-supplemented cost		Variation
		Human	AI	
Quality Assurance Testing	$396,558.21	$93,654.80	$50,000.00	-63.77%
Total	**$396,558.21**	**$143,654.80**		**-63.77%**
Total %	**100.00%**	**23.62%**	**12.61%**	**-63.77%**

QA	Human-only output	AI-supplemented output
Output	1	2.7605
Productivity gains		176.05%

QA output	Human-only Human cost & output	AI-supplemented Human cost & output	AI-supplemented Machine cost	AI-supplemented Machine output
Value 1	$396,558.21	$93,654.80	$50,000	$302,903.41
Ratio 1	100.00%	23.62%	12.61%	76.38%
Ratio AI-sup	276.05%	**65.19%**	34.81%	**210.86%**

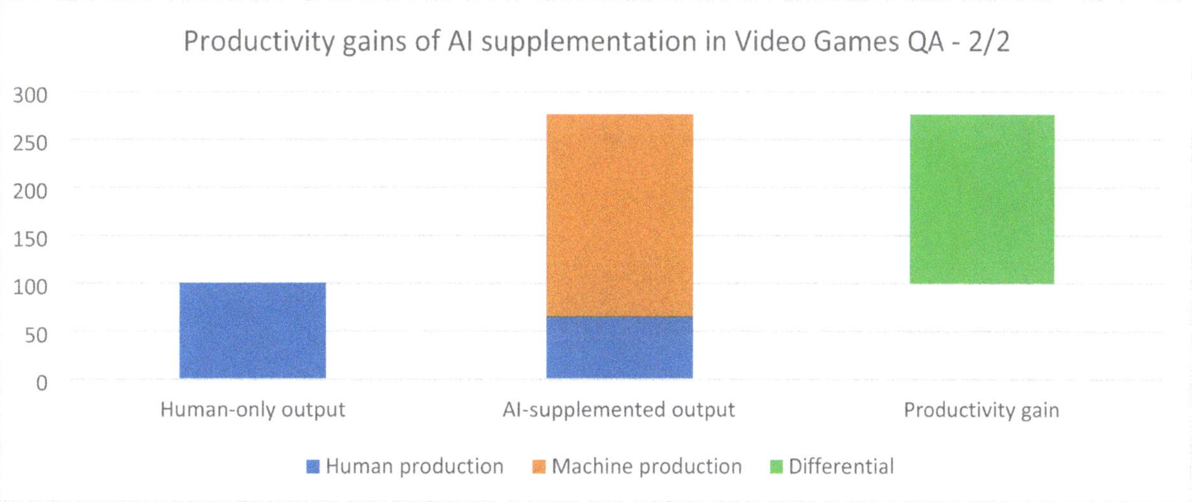

For the sake of this analysis, to have an equivalent comparative and to stay conservative, we will only consider the first-generated cost efficiency and productivity gain AI QA values for our results tally.

(referring to using Gen AI in QA) "I think that the optimization, the cost savings there, are absolutely immense if we can get that working. I'd be hoping we could be looking at 30 to 50% savings there."

—Interview with Jamie Campbell
Founder of MTX Solutions, Co-Founder of d3t Studio, ex-ATI (AMD), ex-Technical Director at THQ

6.6 LOCALIZATION

Game localization is the broader translation process from one language to another. It' the process of adapting a product to make it suitable for another region. Game localization lets a publisher or developer reach new markets. It does this by adapting the game to another language and culture.

Localizing a game can be time-consuming, costly, and prone to errors. However, the application of AI in localization has the potential to revolutionize the game industry, improving efficiency and accuracy.

> *"I think there are different phases. The phase we were in uses the traditional studio model, with very little technology. Like transcribing things by hand, translating things by hand, recording things by hand. [...] That is obviously the most expensive, the least efficient."*
>
> —Interview with Tim Lupo
> Co-founder & CEO of Deeptune, Forbes 30 Under 30 2024

Game localization includes text translation, target language voiceovers (dubbing), local cultural and legal adaptation, and localization testing (LQA).

Localization typically accounts for 0-5% of a game development budget, if present, as outlined in the breakdown below. The actual split can vary based on the game and design choices, such as whether the developers included voiceovers, or if a team decided to localize the game at all. [83,84,85,86]

Game localization budget	Low %	High %
Text Localization	40%	80%
Localized Voiceovers (LOC VO)	0%	50%
Localization QA (LQA)	10%	20%

Below's a typical allocation built on a 3% audio budget allocation for a $10 million project.

Game localization budget	%	$

[83] Three Must-Ask Questions about the Cost of Localizing a Game, LangLink, https://langlinking.com/three-must-ask-questions-about-the-cost-of-localizing-a-game/, 26 July 2022

[84] Breaking Down the Cost of Game Localization, Naarg, https://www.naargmedia.com/cost-of-game-localization/, visited July 2024

[85] Demystifying Game Localization Costs: A Comprehensive Guide, Transphere, https://www.transphere.com/game-localization-costs/, 25 April 2024

[86] The 3 main factors to calculate the game localization cost in 2023!, Sherif Abuizd, https://translationpartner.com/game-localization-cost/, visited July 2024

Text Localization	60%	$180,000
Localized Voiceovers (LOC VO)	25%	$75,000
Localization QA (LQA)	15%	$45,000
Total	**100%**	**$300,000**

> *"What does a world look like where voice recording cost the same as what is the translation cost? Quality expectation from the audience is still high though, so you need to proofread and approve the content, because AI can hallucinate."*
>
> —Interview with Andrea Ballista
> Founder & CEO, Voiseed

Per this budget and the cost efficiencies explained in the following subsections, we can extrapolate a 44% cost-effectiveness of using AI in game localization, and a productivity gain of 79%.

High end AA – LOC cost	Human-only cost	AI-supplemented cost		Variation
		Human	AI	
Text Localization (Text LOC)	$180,000	$108,000	$100	-39.94%
Localized VOs (LOC VO)	$75,000	$30,000	$3,960	-54.72%
Localization QA (LQA)	$45,000	$13,500	$11,786	-43.81%
Total	**$300,000**	**$151,500**	**$15,846**	**-44.22%**
Total	**$300,000**	**$167,346**		**-44.22%**
Total %	**100.00%**	**50.50%**	**5.28%**	**-44.22%**

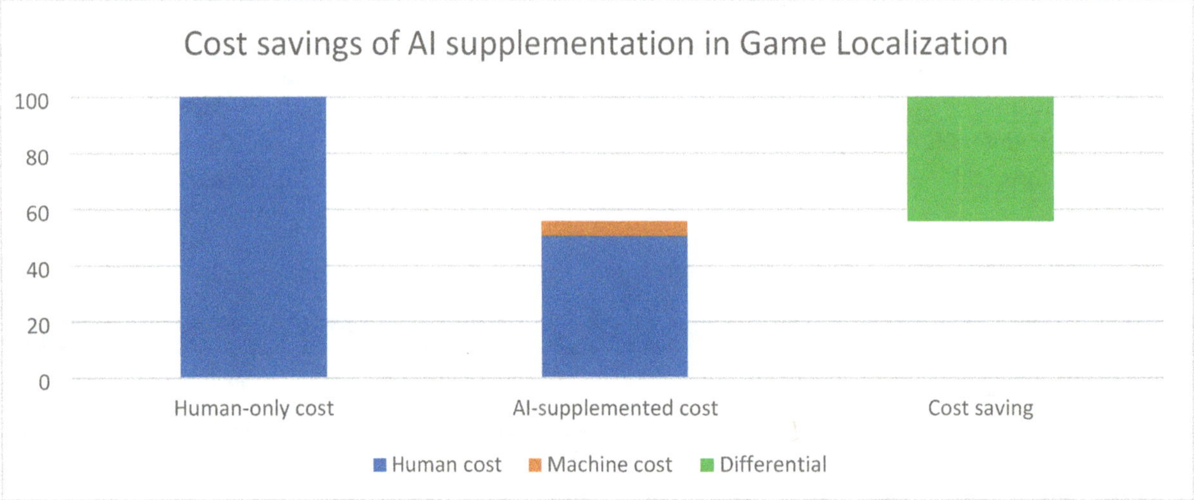

High end AA – LOC Output	Human-only output	AI-supplemented output
Output	1	1.7927
Productivity gains		**79.27%**

High end AA – LOC output	Human-only Human cost & output	AI-supplemented Human cost & output	AI-supplemented Machine cost	AI-supplemented Machine output
Value 1	$300,000	$151,500	$15,846	$148,500
Ratio 1	100.00%	50.50%	5.28%	49.50%
Ratio AI-sup	179.27%	**90.53%**	9.47%	**88.74%**

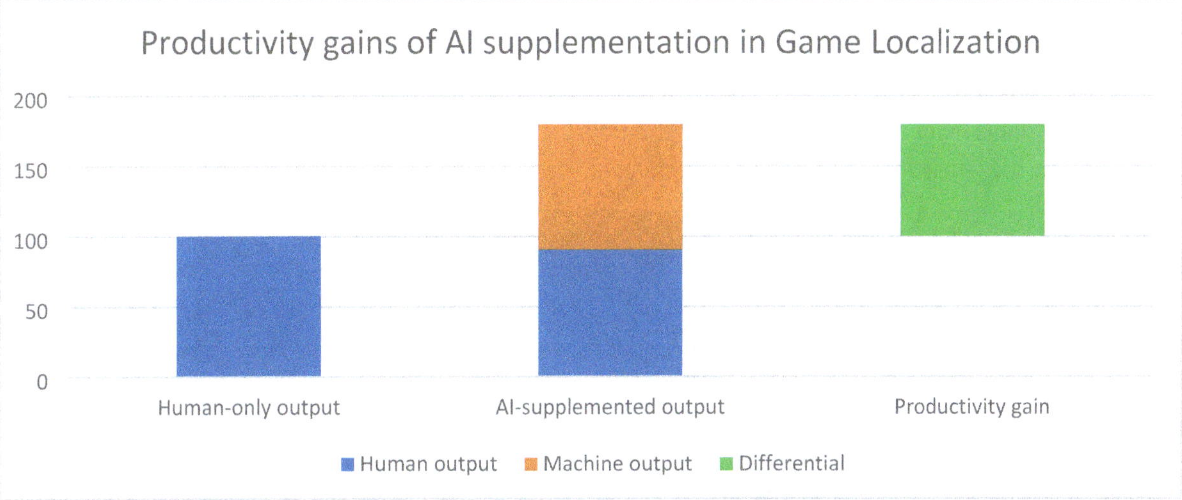

> *"If we can generate an "acceptable" source version without having human in the studio, then we can easily machine translate and generate the other languages applying the same emotional map applied on the script to regenerate the translated script lines even preserving the same casting choices for all the languages. So the "localization" is changing its meaning becoming "multilingual generation" starting from same prompt set, something like what is happening with tools like ChatGPT today."*
>
> —Interview with Andrea Ballista
> Founder & CEO, Voiseed

6.6.1 Text localization

Text localization (Text LOC) involves translating and adapting a game's content to suit different target languages and cultures. It often involves more than just translation. It requires attention to cultural nuances, idioms, and contexts. Localization specialists must ensure the translated text maintains the original tone and intent while resonating with the target audience. They must also address technical challenges, such as text length restrictions, that affect user interface design and display.

You can simplify in-game text translation to a three-step process.

1. Translation: Converting text from one source language to another target language.
2. Proofreading: Second opinion and quality control of translation.
3. Editing: Adapting the translated text to the new receiving format.

Note that not all three of these steps are necessary for every text localization process, and the extent of each can be customized to the required level of quality expected and needed in a game.

Text localization is expected to be one of the most AI-disrupted and soon-to-be automated game processes, but these assumptions have some caveats.

"Essayer de faire quelque chose qui n'est pas en anglais est très difficile. Il n'y a pas assez de data."

AI translation: "Trying to do something that's not in English is very difficult. There's not enough data."

—Interview with Stéphanie Bouchard
Freelance Game Designer/Director - Oxitocyn
Ex Leadership & AI positions at Stockholm Syndrome.AI, Red Barrels, WBGM, Ubisoft, THQ
Ex Game Teacher at NAD-UQAC, Campus ADN, Champlain College, Dawson College
Research contributor at MIT and Concordia University

Traditional translation methods rely on human translators, who can be slow, expensive, and inconsistent. AI-supported translation can process large volumes of text quickly, accurately, and consistently, thereby reducing the time and cost associated with the localization process. Advances in machine learning and natural language processing (NLP) have significantly improved AI translation. A study by researchers at the University of Edinburgh, presented at the 2019 Conference on Machine Translation (MT), found that AI translation can now match the performance of human translators in specific language pairs. In the selected pairs, the average BLEU scores were 0.35 for AI and 0.33 for humans (Barrault et al., 2019). BLEU stands for Bilingual Evaluation Understudy. It is an algorithmic metric to evaluate machine translation quality. The output value indicates how effectively a machine translates text from one language to another. Quality and value are assessed on how close a machine translation is to a human on a scale of 0 to 1. The higher, the better. As a note, it is very rare for human translators themselves to reach 1, and it is almost impossible to do so consistently.

This study compared 153 submissions from 35 institutional models and 5 anonymized MT systems against 1,706 human translators. The study, conducted 5 years ago, already found that many language pairs had technology on par with the average translator's performance, accuracy, and, more importantly, quality. Note that for this study, the quality of translators was mid-to-high level, as researchers removed data from non-reliable workers in all language pairs. The comparative quality bar was high.

Five years ago, the quality was such that, in a multi-step localization process like in the video game industry (Translation → Proofreading → Editing → Localization QA), one could argue that the first step, translation, could be nearly fully automated already. Some localization experts may warn against the negative quality impact of taking such a decision, but:

1. A multi-step verification process with proofreading done by humanswould enable us to identify and correct most introduced MT issues, thereby reducing the risk of such issues being released to the market.
2. The quality benchmark for the entertainment industry isn't as critical as in other industries (e.g., medical, legal, or engineering), and minor issues are often more easily accepted or ignored by their target audiences.
3. The quality output of MT for the most popular language pairs appears to be comparable to human translation when the right mix of localization algorithms is employed.

Furthermore, and regarding the latter, at the AMTA 2022 conference, Marco Trombetti, CEO of Translated, presented the performance gap between expert human translators and optimized machine translation. His data came from 2 billion translation sentences, MT models, and over 136,000 translators. The gap is calculated based on "Time to Edit" (TTE), which represents the average time a translator spends proofreading and editing per word. The argument is that TTE provides a better comparative and quantitative assessment than BLEU and other types of scores. The shorter the review time, the better. Where a human proofreader reviews a human translator's work, they spend, on average, 1 second per word. [87]

The performance gap between human and machine translation has been decreasing steadily and linearly since 2014, when the metric started to be tracked. If the trend continues, machine translation quality should fully match human translators' work before 2030. If linearity continues, we should even expect MT output quality to surpass that of the average human translator by 2030, and see a diminishing need for humans in the loop for translation work before 2040.

[87]This Is the Speed at Which We Are Approaching Singularity in AI, Translated, https://translated.com/speed-to-singularity, visited June 2024

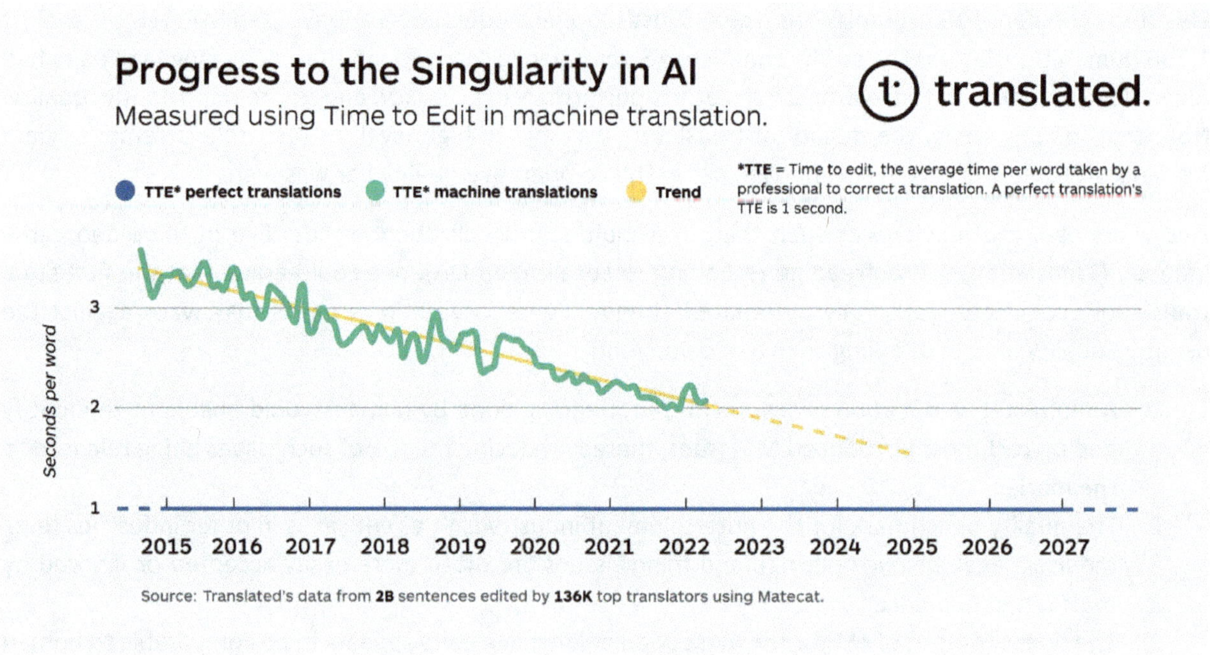

One might expect that gains in this field would be regressive, with marginal gains declining over time. But the Translated team's analysis shows constant, linear progress. The team assumes that this linear progression is explained by Moore's Law (computing power more than doubling every 2 years), the amount of data available for localization purposes online (which is growing at a compounded 6.2% per year), and machine learning algorithms' efficiency getting exponentially better every year (OpenAI reporting 44x improvements between 2012 and 2019).[88,89,90]

Furthermore, language is, by far, the AI domain with the most development to date, and we should expect this trend to continue for some time. Below, visual data representing the domains of notable artificial intelligence systems by year of publication (1950-2023).[91]

---

[88] Cramming more components onto integrated circuits, Moore, Gordon E., Stanford, http://cva.stanford.edu/classes/cs99s/papers/moore-crammingmorecomponents.pdf, April 19th 1965

[89] The 2024 NIMDZI 100,Nimdzi, https://www.nimdzi.com/nimdzi-100-top-lsp/, June 2024

[90] AI and efficiency, Danny Hernandez, Tom Brown,OpenAI, https://openai.com/index/ai-and-efficiency/, 5 May 2020

[91] Domain of notable artificial intelligence systems, by year of publication, Our World in Data, https://ourworldindata.org/grapher/domain-notable-artificial-intelligence-systems?facet=entity&uniformYAxis=1, 1 October 2024

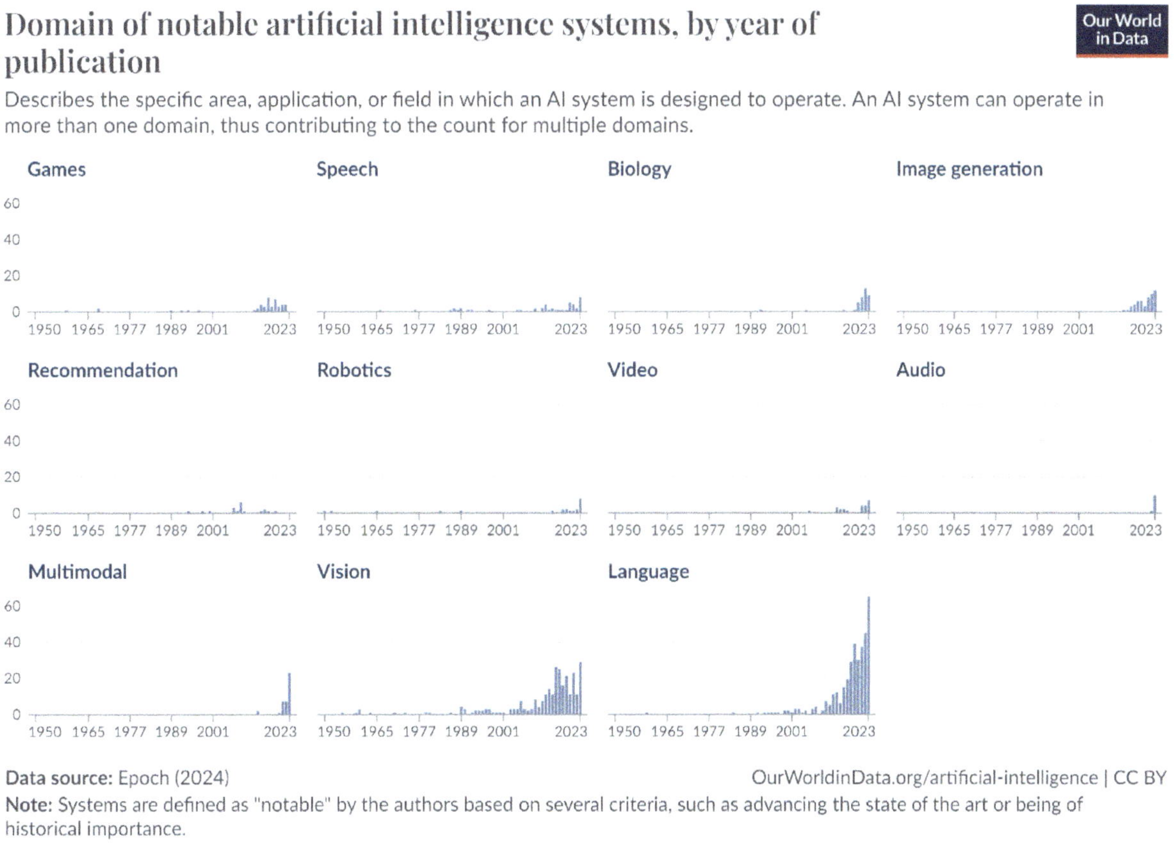

The average cost of human translation is $0.12 per word. This would be for an average to good translator scoring approximately 98% on a multidimensional quality metrics review, specifically in an industry such as gaming. Proofreading costs about half of that, at $0.06 per word. Editing, if needed, costs approximately one-third, at $0.04 per word. For a grand total of $0.22 per word for average human-driven game text localization. [92,93]

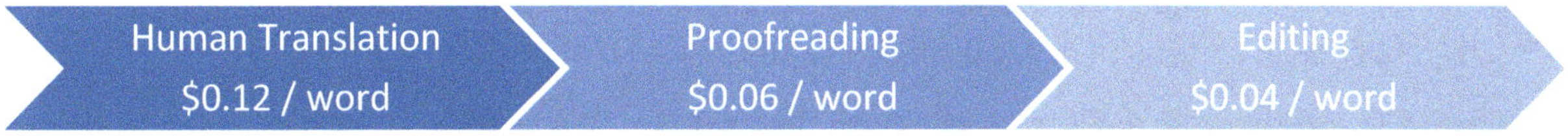

Machine translation engines powered by Google, Amazon, and Microsoft are charging between $0.00001 and $0.00002 per character. Based on research from Peter Norvig, Director of Research at Google, the average word length is 4.79 characters. Gitnux Market data from 2024 on Language and Linguistics Statistics indicates that the average word length in English is 5.1 characters. [94,95]

---

[92] Your Guide to Translation Cost Analysis in 2023, Smartling, https://www.smartling.com/resources/101/translation-rates/, 17 July 2023

[93] Localization Pricing, Allcorect Game content studio, https://allcorrectgames.com/localization-pricing/, visited July 2024

[94] English Letter Frequency Counts: Mayzner Revisited, Peter Norvig, , https://norvig.com/mayzner.html, 2013

[95] Comparing Average Word Length Across Different Languages and Contexts, Gitnux, https://gitnux.org/average-word-length/, 17 July 2024

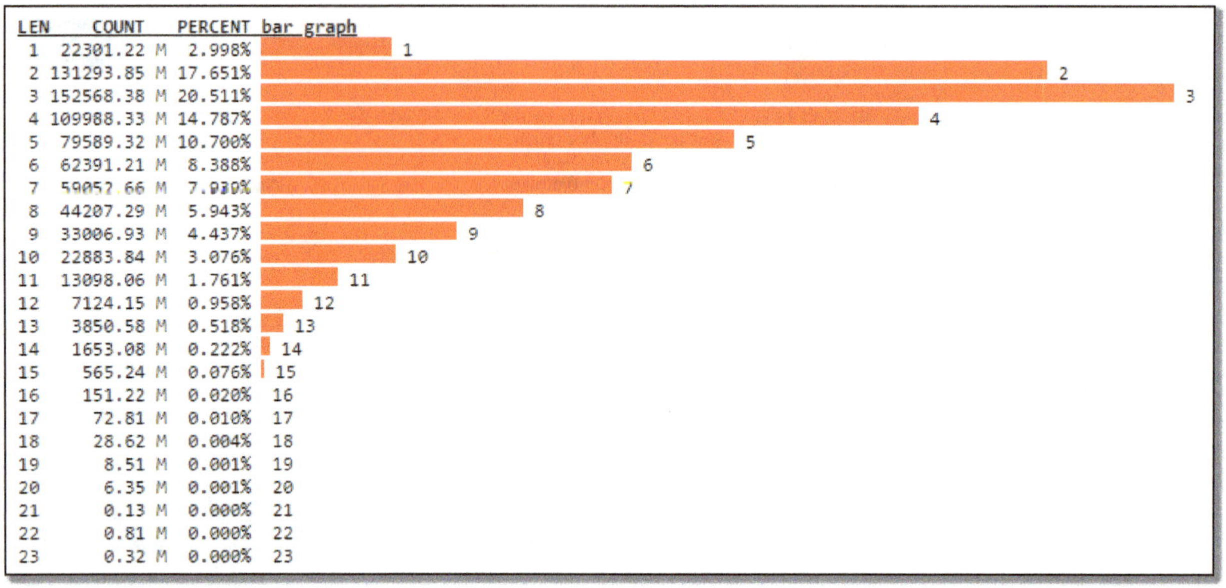

Based on this information, assuming an average of 5 characters per word, as per an English source language, we calculate a translation rate ranging from $0.00005 to $0.0001 per word. Even using the latter value to be conservative, we end up with a relatively free translation step. The AI-supported work would cost less than a thousandth of its original human-only counterpart.

In 2022, Translated's research found that a proofreader needed to spend 1 second per word for human translations and 2 seconds per word for machine translations. We could eliminate translation costs entirely, but we should expect to nearly double the cost of proofreading in 2024 to achieve similar quality results and compensate for the errors introduced by machine translation. Assuming continued improvements in MT linearity, we should expect to be around 1.8 TTE seconds per word for automated translation in 2024, which is 80% more time, effort, and cost required to achieve similar quality in proofreading compared to human-only processes. Making this change would eliminate most of the first translation step cost, but would also raise proofreading costs from $0.06 per word to $0.108 (+80%). The full game text localization process cost would still be reduced from $0.22 per word to $0.1481 per word. A 32.7% reduction in costs, with negligible machine translation costs.

Text Loc cost per word	Human-only cost	AI-supplemented cost	Variation
Translation	$0.12	$0.00	-100%
Proofreading	$0.06	$0.108	+80%
Editing	$0.04	$0.04	-
AI/Tool cost	N/A	$0.0001	-
Total	**$0.22**	**$0.1481**	**-32.7%**

Most game text localization processes use LQA as part of their work. As such, they skip a separate editing step since LQA includes it. Doing so would reduce the game text localization cost from an average $0.18 per word to $0.1081 per word; a 39.9% cost efficiency, delivering a 66.5% productivity gain.

Text Loc cost per word	Human-only cost	AI-supplemented cost	Variation
Translation	$0.12	$0.00	-100%
Proofreading	$0.06	$0.108	+80%
AI/Tool cost	N/A	$0.0001	-
Total	**$0.18**	**$0.1081**	**-39.9%**

Text Localization	Human-only output	AI-supplemented output
Output	1	1.6651
Productivity gains		**66.51%**

A $180,000 text localization project entailing 125,000 words localized in 8 languages (1,000,000 translated words total) would be represented this way.

Text Loc cost per word	Human-only cost	AI-supplemented cost	Variation
Translation	$120,000	$0	-100%
Proofreading	$60,000	$108,000	+80%
AI/Tool cost	N/A	$100	-
Total	**$180,000**	**$108,100**	**-39.9%**

"I think we're now in phase two, which has people are augmenting the traditional dubbing workflow with useful tools which make it go faster. Instead of captioning themselves, they will use a transcription service. Instead of translating it themselves, they'll let GPT do the first draft. [...] AI speeds up the work by 2 to 4x, which is then passed to the customer as 50-75% savings."

—Interview with Tim Lupo
Co-founder & CEO of Deeptune, Forbes 30 Under 30 2024

6.6.2 Audio localization (localized voiceovers)

Audio localization (Audio LOC) encompasses the adaptation of all spoken content and sound elements in a game. This mainly involves re-recording voice-overs in target languages. It may also involve adjusting music and sound effects to accommodate cultural preferences. Voice actors are carefully selected to match the original characters' personalities and emotions, and/or to be adapted to the new targeted market. Localizing audio for a game isn't always done, as it is more costly than simple subtitling or not localizing a game at all. As per text localization, an analysis is usually done to ensure voiceovers' return on investment.

Game Audio Localization can be simplified into a four-step process, with the first two usually taking place during text localization.

1. Translation: Converting scripts from one source language to another target language.
2. Proofreading: Second opinion and quality control of translation.
3. Dubbing and Voiceovers: Recording new localized voices.
4. Editing: Adapting and post-production of the new localized audio for game implementation.

Usually, all four steps are needed for audio localization. They ensure a quality that meets the expectations of the target audience. Audio/VO translation and proofreading steps are usually more demanding than simple text localization. Additional factors must be considered when localizing the script, including length limits and lip-syncing.

> *"I think that original language movies will keep humans, but all of the localized dubbing, especially for the huge back catalogues, are going to use AI."*
>
> -Interview with Tim Lupo
> Co-founder & CEO of Deeptune, Forbes 30 Under 30 2024

Here are some typical average VO industry costs per language. Typically, the price of localized voiceovers (VOs) per language tends to be less than the cost of recording the original voiceovers for various reasons. Often, the same voice actors will be reused for different characters to save time and costs. English is the most popular source language, and the cost of living tends to be lower in non-English-speaking countries. Source English VOs often tend to hire more popular actors, who are costlier. Also, having the source VOs as a reference for actors tends to save time and costs on localization voice direction.[96]

Localized VO	Cost per language
Low-end (Indie)	$3,000-$10,000
Mid-tier (AA)	$10,000-$50,000
High-end (AAA)	$50,000-$200,000+

Assuming text localization costs include translation and proofreading, voiceover localization would mostly follow the same processes defined in the previous Audio Voiceovers section, with tools like ElevenLabs'. It would thus have similar AI benefits in cost and productivity. This is even truer, as this step could benefit from voice cloning of the original voiceovers, if the license allows. We could use the original voiceovers as the source to feed the voice cloning models. In this case, though, we should expect that Text-to-Speech would likely be used. It also means that some localized VO content may need to be recorded using

[96] Video Game Voice Over Rates Unveiled, GoLocalise, https://golocalise.com/blog/video-game-voice-over-rates/, visited September 2024

traditional methods. The automated localized content may not convey the desired intonations and emotions as effectively as the source content does in every instance.[97]

> *"I think that in five years, it's inevitable that 99% of the dubbed content will be done so using software primarily, instead of via acting primarily."*
>
> —Interview with Tim Lupo
> Co-founder & CEO of Deeptune, Forbes 30 Under 30 2024

Based on previous calculations and assumptions made, we should expect a 55% cost efficiency and a 121% productivity gain.

Localized VOs	Human-only cost	AI-supplemented cost
Human cost	$75,000	$30,000
AI/Tool cost	$0	$3,960
Total	**$75,000**	**$33,960**
Cost efficiency		-54.72%

Localized VOs	Human-only output	AI-supplemented output
Output	1	2.2085
Productivity gains		**-120.85%**

> *"Depending on the content, our tool can achieve between 30% and 70% of the cost of a traditional production."*
>
> —Interview with Andrea Ballista
> Founder & CEO, Voiseed

6.6.3 Localization quality assurance

Localization testing, also known as localization quality assurance (LQA), is the final step in ensuring that all localized elements of a game meet the required quality and cultural standards. The process involves testing of both the linguistic and technical aspects of a translated and localized game. LQA testers are typically native speakers of the target language and have experience with gaming. They play through the game to identify issues such as mistranslations, cultural inconsistencies, and spelling errors. They also check for contextual accuracy, ensuring translations make sense. LQA catches and corrects errors that may have been missed during the initial text and audio loc process. This provides a polished and culturally appropriate gaming experience for the target audience.

[97] AI Voice Cloning: Clone Your Voice in Minutes, ElevenLabs, https://elevenlabs.io/voice-cloning, visited September 2024

The cost of testing in-game localization is usually proportionate to the amount of source content to localize, the amount of languages that content is localized into, the amount of time and effort needed to reach that localized content in-game, and the developer's/publisher's decisions regarding quality output levels versus costs of doing so. An average LQA project for a high-end AA game of $10,000,000 will cost approximately $50,000, or 0.5% of the full game budget. For the sake of consistency with the predetermined budget, we will go with $45,000.

The business case provided in the previous Quality Assurance section included and applies to LQA.

Currently, developing AI QA agents for LQA alone will often generate a negative ROI. This is due to the high engineering costs associated with AI agents and the need for custom solutions tailored to each game.

Based on the previously provided AI automation estimates of 70% and a weighted AI QA agent cost of 26.19%, we should expect a 44% cost efficiency and a 78% productivity gain from leveraging AI in LQA.

Localization QA	Human-only cost	AI-supplemented cost
Human cost	$45,000	$13,500
AI/Tool cost	$0	$11,786
Total	**$45,000**	**$25,286**
Cost efficiency		**-43.81%**

Localization QA	Human-only output	AI-supplemented output
Output	1	1.7797
Productivity gains		**-77.97%**

"Traditional localization makes sense if we have the source voice production to use as a base to generate the target languages. But if now we can generate the source performance starting from the script and the symbolic emotional prompts, then we can also generate (rather than localize) all the target performance simply applying the same emotional prompt patterns to the translated script..."

—Interview with Andrea Ballista
Founder & CEO, Voiseed

7 Results Summary and Analysis

7.1 Results

Here's a typical game cost breakdown across major development areas. Actual breakdowns vary depending on the size and type of the game, as well as development and publishing choices, team experience, and other factors. This example budget excludes non-development costs, such as marketing, sales, distribution, publishing, customer support, and legal.

Development area budget	Low end %	High end %
Game Design	5%	10%
Engineering[98]	35%	50%
Art	25%	40%
Audio	5%	10%
Quality Assurance	5%	10%
Localization[99]	0%	5%

Below is a typical estimate for a $10 million 3D AA game with localization.

Development area budget	%	Budget
Game Design	6%	$600,000
Engineering	44%	$4,400,000
Art	33%	$3,300,000
Audio	7%	$700,000
Quality Assurance	7%	$700,000
Localization	3%	$300,000
Total	100%	$10,000,000

When applying and weighting the AI cost efficiencies per area determined in this research's analysis, AI supplementation can generate a potential cost savings of 43.27% when applied to game development.

Development area	Human-only cost	AI-supplemented cost		AI-supplemented ratio	
		Human	AI	Human	AI
Game Design	$600,000	$45,000	$3,601	7.50%	0.60%
Engineering	$4,400,000	$3,960,000	$4,681	90.00%	0.11%
Art	$3,300,000	$1,007,482	$25,526	30.53%	0.77%
Audio	$700,000	$95,000	$5,400	13.57%	0.77%
Quality Assurance	$700,000	$343,396	$183,331	49.06%	26.19%
Localization	$300,000	$151,500	$15,846	50.50%	5.28%
Total	**$10,000,000**	**$5,450,877**	**$222,538**	54.51%	2.23%
Total	**$10,000,000**	**$5,673,416**		**56.73%**	

[98] Including early game design prototyping, which could be considered in "Game Design".

[99] Including localized audio voiceovers, which could be considered in "Audio", localization quality assurance, which could be considered in "Quality Assurance".

Here's a simplified, summed-up tally of the previously shown data, and a graphical representation of the calculated cost savings.

Development area	Human-only cost	AI-supplemented cost	AI-supplemented ratio	AI-supplemented Variation
Game Design	$600,000	$48,601.20	8.10%	-91.90%
Engineering	$4,400,000	$3,964,680.85	90.11%	-9.89%
Art	$3,300,000	$1,033,007.25	31.30%	-68.70%
Audio	$700,000	$100,400	14.34%	-85.66%
Quality Assurance	$700,000	$526,726.24	75.25%	-24.75%
Localization	$300,000	$167,346	55.78%	-44.22%
Total	**$10,000,000**	**$5,673,415.54**	**56.73%**	**-43.27%**

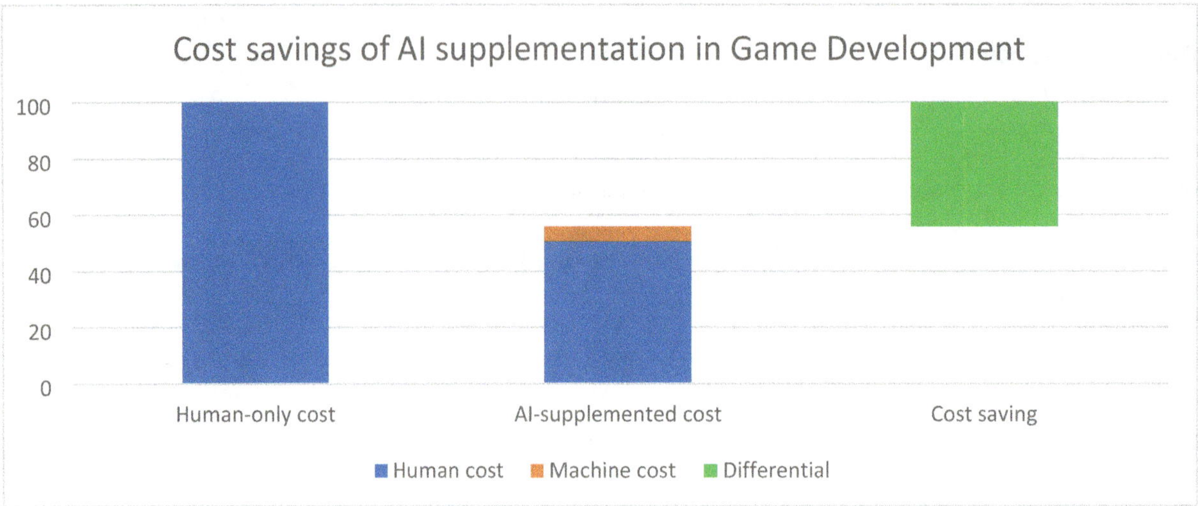

Using the previous cost efficiency data, we can calculate that AI supplementation can generate a potential productivity gain of +76% in game development.

Game Development output	Human-only output	AI-supplemented output
Output	1	1.7626
Productivity gains		**+76.26%**

Game Development output	Human-only Human cost & output	AI-supplemented Human cost & output	AI-supplemented Machine cost	AI-supplemented Machine output
Value 1	$10,000,000	$5,450,877	$222,538	$4,549,123
Ratio 1	100.00%	54.51%	2.23%	45.49%
Ratio AI-sup	176.26%	**96.08%**	3.92%	**80.18%**

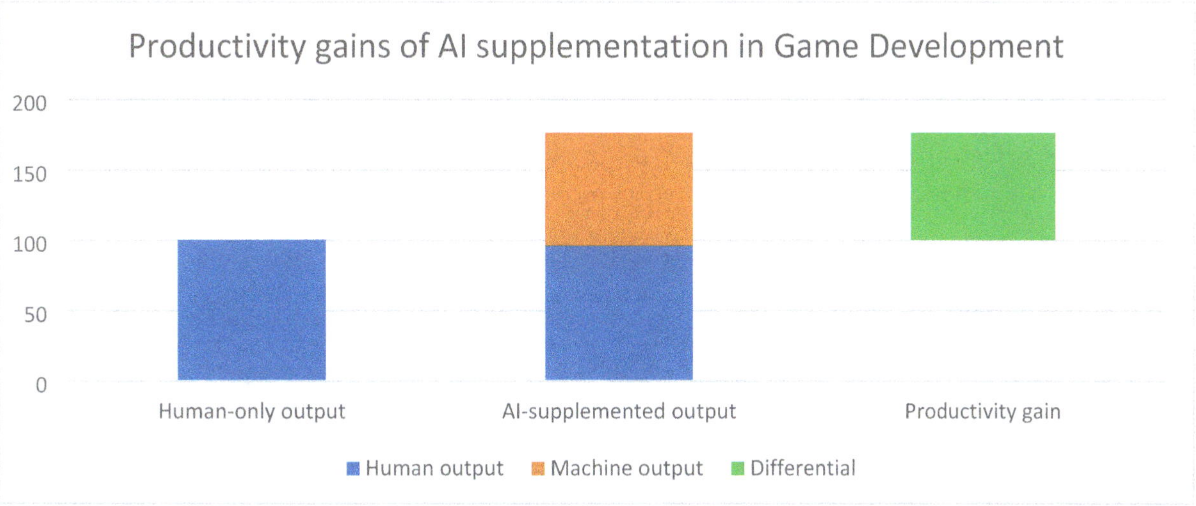

By combining the previous cost and productivity data, we can create a ratio analysis and calculate AI-to-human efficiency ratios. It demonstrates the significant cost efficiency of AI's output compared to human-only output for the solutions evaluated in this analysis. For comparative reasons, assuming that the human output to cost ratio is 1:1, we can simply calculate AI's as such:

AI to Human output Efficiency ratio = AI-supplemented Machine output / Machine cost

where

AI-supplemented Machine output = Human-only Human output - AI-supplemented Human output

Applying AI in the development areas we've evaluated yields AI output to cost ratios ranging from approximately 2x to 154x, with an average of approximately 20x when weighted proportionally against a game budget, compared to human output. This means that, in game development, properly using the AI tools we've reviewed is, on average, 20 times more efficient than not using them, when applied to tasks for which they are best suited.

Development area	Human-only Human cost & output	AI-supplemented Human cost & output	AI-supplemented Machine cost	AI-supplemented Machine output	AI to Human output Efficiency ratio
Game Design	$600,000	$45,000	$3,601	$555,000	154.12
Engineering	$4,400,000	$3,960,000	$4,681	$440,000	94.00
Art	$3,300,000	$1,007,482	$25,526	$2,292,518	89.81
Audio	$700,000	$95,000	$5,400	$605,000	112.04
QA	$700,000	$343,396	$183,331	$356,604	1.95
Localization	$300,000	$151,500	$15,846	$148,500	9.37
Total	$10,000,000	$5,450,877	$222,538	$4,549,123	20.44

Despite the efficiency discrepancy, in a balanced capitalist market economy, we would expect efficiency ratios to be closer to 1.

Here are a few things that these high numbers could convey:

1. There's a low AI adoption rate in the game development field.
2. AI technology is advancing exponentially rapidly, and its application will grow exponentially.
3. There's a high probability of change and disruption in game development.
4. There's a high probability of change in AI game development.

Based on our observations, all of them ring true and support some of our additional key learnings.

"Ça commence à devenir plus sérieux. Des vraies applications professionnelles qui amènent de la valeur. Des outils de productivité. Là, ça devient intéressant."

AI translation: "It's starting to get more serious. Real business applications that add value. Productivity tools. Now it's getting interesting."

—Interview with Pierre-Paul Giroux
Vice-President Engineering A.I. at Unity

"I believe we'll see major productivity gains, but not by refining the way we work today. The real value will come from changing how we work altogether."

—Interview with Stephen Peacock
Director AI at 2K, Ex-Head of AI at AWS & Keywords

Note that QA has an AI efficiency ratio that is significantly lower than that of other services, at just below 2. This makes sense and isn't an anomaly, as the evaluated solution for that specific service was engineer-heavy, had relatively costly customized AI agents, and had solutions tailored to each specific context. The solution proposed is highly optimized for cost efficiency.

Inversely, most other tools evaluated were VC-backed and could be aimed at a "be first, be fast, be big" type of strategy, often trying to reach market share domination before profitability. This would translate to a penetration pricing strategy, where a low price is set to enter and maintain market share in a competitive market, or potentially a competitor-based one, essentially pricing goods and services based on what competitors charge. It could also simply mean that the new technology is very cost-effective when compared to traditional working methods, and we have new AI organizations exploring cost-based pricing. In any case, a balanced market would tend to use value-based pricing more, where the price is set closer to the value a client would benefit from what is bought.

"I don't think we're going to have AI make games. I think we're going to have people make games and they use AI. But no one cares that it's AI. I think the label will go away. I think the buzz will disappear. And in the end, you'll be left with really interesting tools that do really quite amazing things that we never think about.

Shaders are a great example. When I started, it was all fixed function pipeline. You had a standard way of doing it because that's all the video card could do. And then, all of a sudden, you get GPUs and they can perform instructions and do amazing things. And so people figure out we can write all these amazing shaders, and games look phenomenally different."

—Interview with Matt Ditton
CEO and Co-Founder of Mighty Games Group & Mighty Build and Test

7.2 Key learnings

7.2.1 AI efficiency in videogames is mostly limited by AI adoption

"There are many, MANY, barriers to AI adoption in organizations. Many barriers to implement new systems in an already running organization. In many ways, you are better off addressing those than working on the technology itself."

-Interview with Christoffer Holmgård
CEO and Co-Founder of modl.ai

Despite the potential for AI to have a drastic business-changing impact in video games, Goldman Sachs analysts predict that global industry-agnostic productivity improvements from AI will be limited to an average of 1.5% per year. Two factors explain the discrepancy. First, by the differences between industries and how much artificial intelligence can be applied to each. Second, and foremost, by the pace of adoption and integration of AI into day-to-day business processes. [100]

"You've got all of this shiny stuff, and it does all these shiny things, but you have to deal with game studios having legacy ways of working from the last 30 years. There's a habit to the way that everything functions. It permeates the entire structure. There's an approach everyone has that is informally standardized. It takes significant effort or a major crisis to bring change."

—Interview with Matt Ditton
CEO and Co-Founder of Mighty Games Group & Mighty Build and Test

Regarding the first point, and referring to the introductory data, our analysis indicates that the video game industry and its sub-niches predominantly rank among the top 20 percent of the distribution presented in the introductory data. It's no surprise. Most of the gaming industry professions involve data and related creation, and their core components have all been the focus of multiple AI ventures and initiatives. This wouldn't explain why there is a wide gap between the high impact AI can deliver and its currently limited effect in the industry, though.

---

[100] Generative AI could raise global GDP by 7%, Goldman Sachs Research, https://www.goldmansachs.com/insights/articles/generative-ai-could-raise-global-gdp-by-7-percent, 5 April 2023

"There will be bits where AI allows for ridiculous efficiencies. But at the same time, there are people who really like those inefficiencies. They have a mastery of that production style. Getting people to make that change is hard."

—Interview with Matt Ditton
CEO and Co-Founder of Mighty Games Group & Mighty Build and Test

"C'est dur aujourd'hui à faire cette pédagogie-là. Pourtant, je pense qu'elle est essentielle pour arriver à faire en sorte que les gens utilisent les outils."

AI translation: "It's hard to train people. But I think it's essential to get people to use the tools."

—Interview with Félix Balmonet
Co-Founder & CEO, Chat3D

"I think that hardly any studios are leveraging AI automation in game development. I think there will be differences in geographies, for one, not least because of liability and the potential impact of that, but I genuinely think people are in a holding pattern, watching what's happening. Because things don't feel like they're quite there yet, and I think people are waiting for a little bit more reassurance. When it comes to Gen AI application, less than 5% of development studios are leveraging it."

"0 to 5% of studios are using Gen AI. When it comes to automation, like scripting, I would say 90% of studios are using automation, but non-AI based automation."

—Interview with Jamie Campbell
Founder of MTX Solutions, Co-Founder of d3t Studio, ex-ATI (AMD), ex-Technical Director at THQ

> *"It's hard for companies to move forward when large parts of their team are concerned about the ethics, environmental impact, or security of AI. Those concerns are real and they're slowing adoption."*
>
> —Interview with Stephen Peacock
> Director AI at 2K, Ex-Head of AI at AWS & Keywords

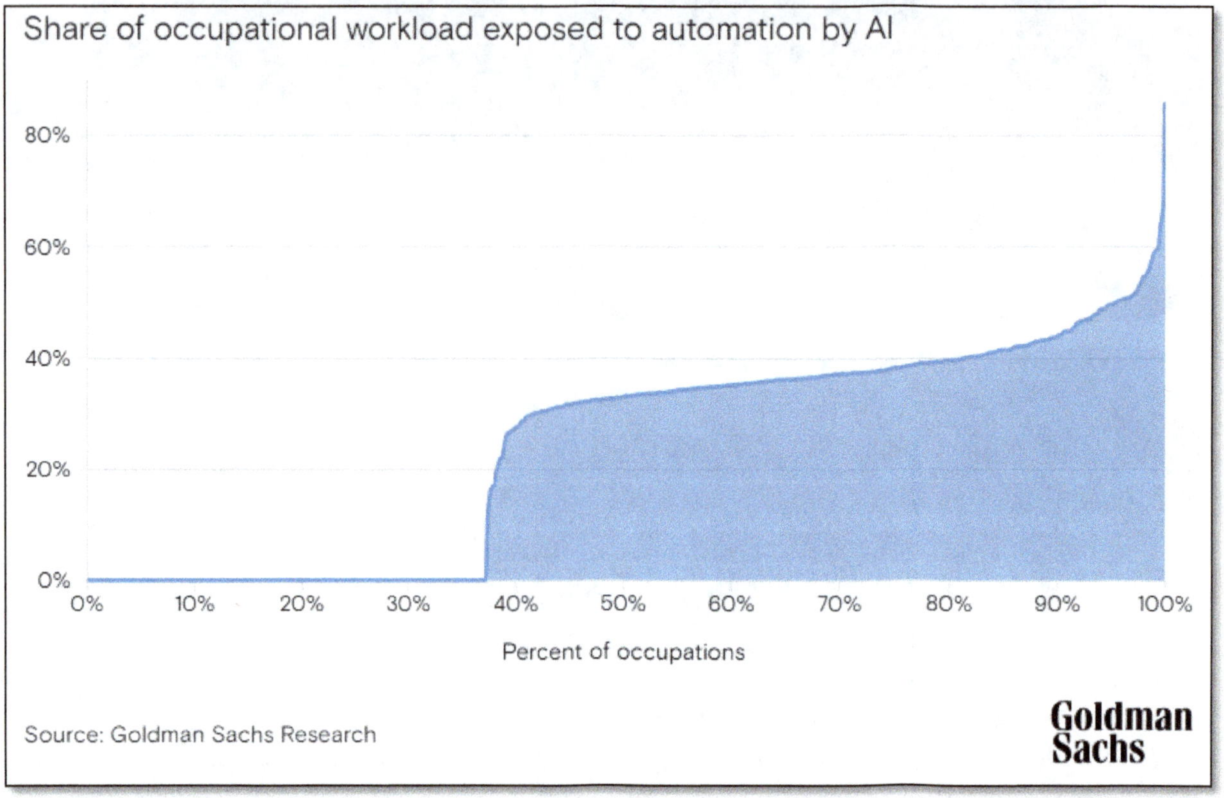

What would explain the discrepancy is that, despite gaming occupational workload being highly exposed to AI automation, there is a slow pace of AI adoption. We believe that this slow pace is multifactorial, with reasons and applications varying greatly from one organization to another and from one individual to another.

> *"There's adoption resistance because of quality. But quality is improving so rapidly that, in a few years, there won't be any AI shortcomings."*
>
> —Interview with Tim Lupo
> Co-founder & CEO of Deeptune, Forbes 30 Under 30 2024

From what we've observed, the tools and techniques for implementing AI in production pipelines are already present and quite efficient; however, people are still largely unaware of them or hesitant to use them in their daily work. There's a lack of awareness and tool use training in most organizations, and the tools are so fresh and rapidly changing that most schools are unable to include them in their curriculums in a timely manner. People don't know what's out there.

> *"If you want to use AI end-to-end for most purposes, the barrier to adoption is not the capability of the AI models. It is the cost and latency associated with using existing foundation models to their fullest, and the integration within current organizational workflows."*
>
> —Interview with Christoffer Holmgård
> CEO and Co-Founder of modl.ai

Many organizations lack the AI talent to use existing tools. Those tools often currently lack a user-friendly interface and require engineering expertise to be leveraged effectively. For example, there are over 1,000,000 AI models on Hugging Face. Many could help organizations, but most people can't use them as they are. They don't know a useful AI programming language for AI, nor the other critical parts to make a model work. These situations can be partially resolved with organizational and individual awareness, AI use, and technical trainings. Strategic hiring will likely also be necessary for most organizations, though.

> *"Only about 1% of game studios leverage AI into game testing... if you're lucky."*
>
> —Interview with Matt Ditton
> CEO and Co-Founder of Mighty Games Group & Mighty Build and Test

"Game developers have always been quite insular. The studios are on lockdown when they're doing development. They don't let technologies in and out easily because they're worried about the leak of their IP or others, and rightly so. Development cycles are also very long. So, adoption rates might be low right now because a whole bunch of games just shipped over the last two years. [...] And live games are live and operating. They won't be making massive changes because they just need to operate those games."

—Interview with Liza Wood
Principal Group Program Manager – Data & AI Leader at Microsoft
Ex-Disney/WB Games/Behavior/EA

On the other side of the spectrum, many organizations feature AI power users... for which many keep their AI use under wraps. Many reasons explain this. Some individuals fear potentially violating company policies, either because the guidelines are unclear, too restrictive, or because they are already in violation of those guidelines by, for example, sharing private company information on their own personal devices. Some others want to keep that competitive advantage for themselves, or fear that if their boss were to know about it, there would be an increased expectation of their workload without compensation. Or worse, that they may be encouraging the automation of their own role, which could bring job insecurity for themselves and their colleagues. In all of these cases, not only is there no incentive for them to share this information, but there's a large incentive not to share it.

"I think that the current level of AI adoption in the market is less than 10%. [...] The interesting thing for me has been how little of this tech has actually made it into production in the industry still."

—Interview with Christoffer Holmgård
CEO and Co-Founder of modl.ai

Organizations need to put incentives in place, such as a reward system, to encourage AI cultural shifts among their employees. "What's in it for me?" is important, and is a two-way street between organizations and employees. There are ways to reach win-win scenarios. Case studies can also be helpful, especially when they come directly from line managers and executives. Once managers become users, they often encourage their own staff to leverage AI and also train them directly on how to do so. Another way to do so is to also track and measure the AI implementation and impact as a company KPI and, as is the case with many KPIs and companies, attribute team and individual performance goals, reviews, and bonuses to that dataset. As the often-misattributed quote says, "What gets measured gets managed".[101]

> *"There is always this not invented here mentality with lots of developers, especially experienced developers, who will look at someone else's code, and they'll look at it, and they'll go, delete that, I'm going to write that again."*
>
> —Interview with Jamie Campbell
> Founder of MTX Solutions, Co-Founder of d3t Studio, ex-ATI (AMD), ex-Technical Director at THQ

There are also some purposely lagging organizations, due to previous AI moratoriums or banning rules, which relate to fears of legal implications or intellectual property leaks, or public relations issues stemming from the perceived job displacement that the technology will generate. On that note, some organizations have publicized that they've banned the use of AI in their game production pipelines. Upon further research, though, many of them have only banned using internal data within external reaching tools in fear of internal data/IP leaks. Or banned using AI creations generated from platforms fed with external data in fear of being later sued for accidental IP infringements. Many of these teams are open to internal-only AI processes, leveraging data they already own or that will be generated by their own employees in the future.

There is both a growing push to change towards AI adoption and a growing resistance to it. Earlier this year, Valve changed its original course and now appears to approve of most AI-generated content, as long as it is disclosed and falls within certain legal guardrails.[102] At the other end of the spectrum, a wave of unionization and strikes is emerging, driven by employees fearing both job displacement and the commoditization of their roles, which could lead to job cuts and market salary reductions.[103,104]

Most of the current potential productivity gains are not stemming from further tool development, but from organizational and individual AI tool adoption. A positive example of this is the case of Mighty Bear's art team mentioned previously, which quadrupled its output once it decided to embrace AI efficiency.[105]

---

[101] AI in organizations: Some tactics, Ethan Mollick, https://www.oneusefulthing.org/p/ai-in-organizations-some-tactics, 4 October 2024

[102] AI Content on Steam, Valve, https://steamcommunity.com/groups/steamworks/announcements/detail/3862463747997849619, 9 January 2024

[103] Video game performers strike over concerns about AI, Johny Walfisz, Euronews, https://www.euronews.com/culture/2024/07/26/video-game-performers-strike-over-concerns-about-ai, 26 July 2024

[104] AI Clash Stalls Labor Talks for Video Game Actors, Producers, Ian Kullgren, Bloomberg Law, https://news.bloomberglaw.com/daily-labor-report/ai-clash-stalls-labor-talks-for-video-game-actors-producers, 29 August 2024

[105] How the Use of AI Evolved Our Art Production Pipelines, Mario Toon, Mighty Bear, https://www.mightybeargames.com/post/how-the-use-of-ai-evolved-our-art-production-pipelines, 25 October 2023

> *"Giving a team access to a state-of-the-art LLM doesn't improve productivity on day one. In fact, it often slows things down at first. People experiment with the tool, but it takes time before they start using it in ways that genuinely save time."*
>
> —Interview with Stephen Peacock
> Director AI at 2K, Ex-Head of AI at AWS & Keywords

This may also translate to great outliers and a greater performance disparity between organizations in the gaming industry and others. Companies and individuals that rapidly adopt AI for most of their processes may quickly and significantly outperform those that lag behind in AI adoption. There's a now-common saying, popularized by Karim Lakhani, Harvard Business School professor: "AI is not going to replace humans, but humans with AI are going to replace humans without AI.".

The following is a brief, non-exhaustive list of AI adoption limiting factors and potential solutions, based on the information presented in this section.

AI Adoption limiting factor & solutions	AI awareness training	AI use training	Provide proven prompts	AI technical training	AI Engineering hiring	AI Collaboration	Phased AI implementation	AI company guidelines	Incentivise AI workflows	Case study sharing	AI benchmarks	Build own AI tools	Adapt existing AI models	...
Lack of AI awareness	√	√	√			√	√	√	√	√	√			
Lack of AI training	√	√	√	√		√			√	√				
Lack of AI engineering	√	√		√	√	√			√					
Restrictive company guidelines	√	√	√	√		√	√	√	√	√	√	√	√	
Missing company guidelines	√	√	√	√		√		√	√	√	√			
Regulatory/Legal uncertainty	√	√	√	√		√	√	√		√	√	√	√	
Security and IP uncertainty	√	√	√	√		√	√	√		√	√	√	√	
Dev integration challenges	√	√		√	√	√	√		√	√	√	√	√	
Lack of user-friendly tools	√	√	√	√	√	√				√		√	√	
Lack of industry-specific tools	√	√	√	√	√	√				√		√	√	
...														

"These tools are like discovering fire for the first time. Right now, we're mostly getting burned or distracted by the shadows on the wall. It will take time before we figure out how to turn this into engines, infrastructure, and tools that truly drive progress. Generative AI is still at the very beginning."

—Interview with Stephen Peacock
Director AI at 2K, Ex-Head of AI at AWS & Keywords

"Pour l'art, il y a encore plus de studios qui l'empêchent, (à cause des risques légaux) alors on est à l'opposé. On doit être dans le 10-20% d'application. [...] Quand je parle de Sprite Generation, j'ai du pushback à cause du IP infringement."

AI translation: "For art, there are even more studios that prevent it, (because of the legal risks) so we're at the opposite end of the spectrum. We're probably in the 10-20% application range. [...] When I talk about Sprite Generation, I get pushback because of IP infringement."

—Interview with Pierre-Paul Giroux
Vice-President Engineering A.I. at Unity

"I don't believe that AI will come and make sudden sweeping changes. [...] It's incredibly hard to find people who are very happy to try something else. A want for change or untested things is very low. Risk is not something anybody wants, and unknown new things are risky. It's likely why the potential for change is incredibly high with these products, but the implementation of these changes is incredibly low.

—Interview with Matt Ditton
CEO and Co-Founder of Mighty Games Group & Mighty Build and Test

7.2.2 AI and its application will continue to evolve increasingly rapidly, in and out of games

> *"Things are coming out so fast, even in Hugging Face. Hugging Face is the hub of open-source AI, and we can't keep up with everything. People inside are surprised already. We don't even have time to catch up with all the things coming out so fast. So just the speed of it is a surprise."*
>
> —Interview with Dylan Ebert, PhD
> Developer Advocate Engineer, Hugging Face

Every year, new pundits claim that Moore's Law is dead. Every year, they are proven wrong. Not only do humans keep finding new and innovative ways to keep the law alive, but we also create new ways of using computers and AI (e.g., chain-of-thought prompting and self-consistency techniques), and even new

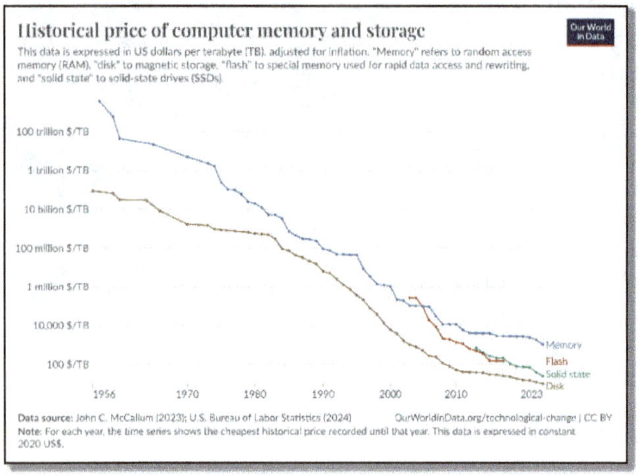

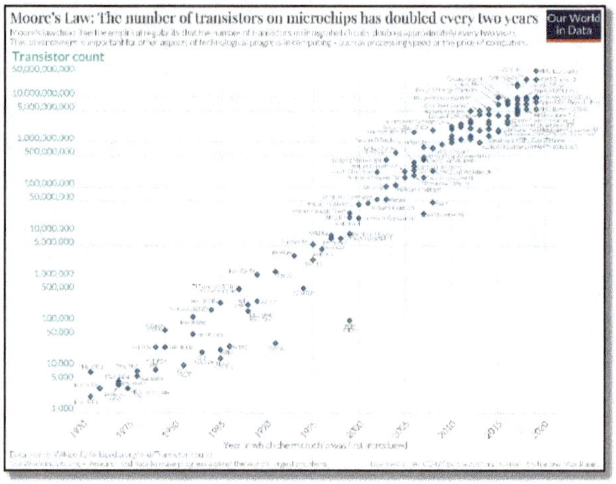

computers entirely (e.g., quantum computing) that push the limits of computational power even further than what Gordon E. Moore would have predicted. Similarly, computer costs, as have AI token costs, have decreased exponentially, allowing further improvements and applications. [106]

[106] What is Morre's Law?, Max Roset et al., Our Wolrd in Data, https://ourworldindata.org/moores-law, 8 March 2023

> *"Ce qu'on a trouvé absolument dingue, c'est le changement de fusil d'épaule de plein de boîtes qui, initialement, ne voulaient pas du tout en faire, et se sont maintenant mis à en faire à fond."*
>
> *AI translation: "What we've found crazy is the 180° of companies that initially didn't want to do it at all, and have now started doing it all the way."*
>
> —Interview with Félix Balmonet
> Co-Founder & CEO, Chat3D

Technology has grown exponentially throughout our history, computers included, and AI will continue to do so. This presents tremendous possibilities and opportunities for us. We may be on the cusp of a technological boon that supports the gaming industry and helps humanity like never before.

There are also obvious risks to this. What happens when technology grows so rapidly and new tools come out so fast that people, businesses, if not whole industries, don't have the time to react? Training and other AI adoption techniques will help. However, the rapid changes will likely induce disruption from one industry to another.

> *"I'm working with people who've been, like myself, in technology our entire careers, and we're surprised at how fast it's moving."*
>
> —Interview with Liza Wood
> Principal Group Program Manager – Data & AI Leader at Microsoft
> Ex-Disney/WB Games/Behavior/EA

"J'ai l'impression qu'il y a un ralentissement ces temps-ci. Je pense que la vitesse des LLMs a été démesuré dans les dernières années. Je pense qu'avec un GPT4o on va pouvoir se rendre loin. Le modèle de base fondationnel, il n'aura plus tant besoin d'évoluer. Je pense que la vrai magie est au niveau des applications. Avec la même base qu'on a avec un 4o, on va pouvoir faire beaucoup plus de choses qu'on s'imagine présentement."

AI translation: "I feel like there's a slowdown these days. I think the speed of LLMs has been a bit crazy in the last few years. I think that with GPT4o, we'll be able to go a long way. The basic foundation model won't need to evolve so much. I think the real magic is in the applications. With the same base we have with a 4o, we're going to be able to do a lot more things than we currently imagine."

—Interview with Pierre-Paul Giroux
Vice-President Engineering A.I. at Unity

"Pour les Gen AI et les Transformers, ce qui va être intéressant, c'est vrai qu'on est à court de data à capturer, mais on va tomber avec du data synthétique. L'une des prochaines batailles, c'est la génération de data synthétique. Ça, je pense que pour l'art, pour les films, pour ces choses-là, je pense que ça va être vraiment intéressant parce que là, il va y avoir un effet boule de neige."

AI translation: "For Gen AI and Transformers, it's true that we're running out of data to capture, but what's going to be interesting is that we're going to come down with synthetic data. One of the next battles is the generation of synthetic data. I think that for art, for films, for these types of things, it's going to be really interesting because there's going to be a snowball effect."

—Interview with Pierre-Paul Giroux
Vice-President Engineering A.I. at Unity

7.2.3 Many industries are set to be disrupted, and many markets will transform

Since 2015, LLMs have begun to perform as well as, and in some cases outperform, humans on various tests, and the pace of new improvements continues to grow.[107,108] What will happen when a rapidly growing number of AI models are able to supplement, if not replace, human tasks? What will happen when they are able to replace whole industries?

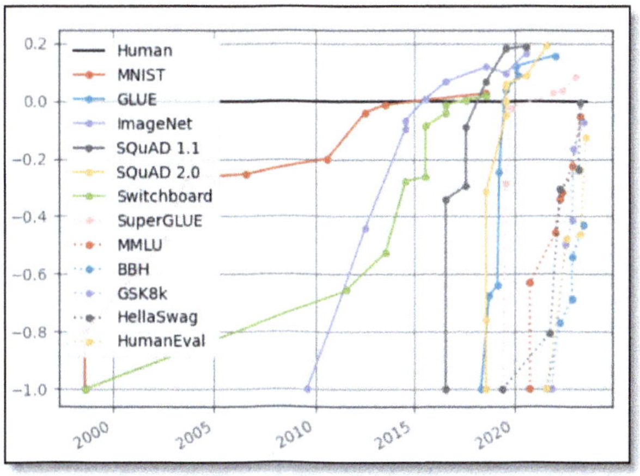

The rapid change in technology and the sudden appearance of new AI tools and players in the field will have some impacts. Here are some assumed outcomes.

> *"The current AI trend is really helping capital raising, but also client-readiness and client adoption of AI. Clients didn't believe that the technology could do what it could 2-3 years ago. They've turned around and now expect really advanced AI behaviors, designed for their specific use-case, out of the box."*
>
> —Interview with Christoffer Holmgård
> CEO and Co-Founder of modl.ai

B2C Games product volume increase and price reduction

The advent of lower-cost production via AI, or more production for the same cost, should reduce the entry barrier to developing and publishing games, thus increasing the volume of available titles. Game production cost reductions and the subsequent increase in game volume should lead to an overall decrease in average game prices.

Considering the drastic potential efficiency gain of using AI in game development, it's possible that we will see a B2C games product flood, but this would go against our current findings that, despite the technology being available, most organizations are not leveraging that technology to its full potential and are only adopting it very slowly.

---

[107] Dynabench: Rethinking Benchmarking in NLP, Douwe Kiela et al., NAACL 2021, https://arxiv.org/abs/2104.14337, 7 April 2021

[108] Plotting Progress in AI, Douwe Kiela, https://contextual.ai/news/plotting-progress-in-ai/, 31 July 2023

> *"Si on tient à garder la structure de production de jeux présente, on va seulement avoir une utilisation (IA) marginale, dans des contextes très spécifiques."*
>
> *AI translation: "If we want to keep the present game production structure, we're only going to have marginal (AI) use, in very specific contexts."*
>
> —Interview with Stéphanie Bouchard
> Freelance Game Designer/Director - Oxitocyn
> Ex Leadership & AI positions at Stockholm Syndrome.AI, Red Barrels, WBGM, Ubisoft, THQ
> Ex Game Teacher at NAD-UQAC, Campus ADN, Champlain College, Dawson College
> Research contributor at MIT and Concordia University

B2C Indie and AA Games product volume increase, faster than AAA

AI's application and efficiency are greater on lower complexity outputs. Considering this, we should expect Indie and AA (smaller/simpler games) AI application, adoption, and ROI to increase faster than for AAA (large and complex games). It will become, at least temporarily, safer and more lucrative for both game developers and publishers who leverage AI to focus on Indie and AA games rather than larger AAA ones.

The caveat would be if there's a market flooding of Indie and AA games, partly because of AI. In those cases, AAA may partly benefit as their size and complexity become a market differentiator.

"Unity a fait que c'est facile de faire des jeux. Moi, quand j'étais jeune, faire un jeu, il fallait que tu partes et que tu écrives à main. Tu partais de là et il fallait que tu parles à ta carte graphique. Faire un jeu avec une gang de chums, ça ne se faisait pas. Avec Unity, Unreal, Godot, c'est rendu vraiment facile de faire un jeu. Le downside, c'est qu'il va y avoir du shovelware, du crapware, des jeux poche de moindre qualité qui vont sortir. Ça va floader le marché. [...] Pour moi, AI c'est la même chose. "

AI translation: "Unity has made it easy to make games. When I was younger, making a game, you had to go out and write by hand. You'd start from there and you'd have to talk to your graphics card. You couldn't make a game with a bunch of friends. With Unity, Unreal and Godot, making a game has become really easy. The downside is shovelware, crapware and lesser-quality games coming out. That's going to flood the market. [...] For me, AI is the same thing. "

—Interview with Pierre-Paul Giroux
Vice-President Engineering A.I. at Unity

Pressure on Game Publishers' profitability

The advent of lower-cost production via AI, or more production for the same cost, should reduce the entry barrier to developing and publishing games, thus reducing the financial dependency and risk of publishing a game. This, in turn, should mean that we should see an increase in the number of game developers self-publishing titles, without needing financial or service aid from larger publishers. This is even more true considering that larger game organizations appear to be lagging behind in AI adoption compared to smaller studios. This effect may be partly mitigated by the fact that the available technology will likely encourage both developers and publishers to create larger and more complex games. [109]

---

[109] GDC State of the Game Industry 2023 report, GDC, January 2024, https://reg.gdconf.com/state-of-game-industry-2024

"I think the biggest loss is a little more meta in that it makes it much easier to make games, and it disrupts the traditional structure of game development, but in a way that is kind of good and bad. I think it's way better for indie game developers than it is for AAA, that's for sure."

—Interview with Dylan Ebert, PhD
Developer Advocate Engineer, Hugging Face

The increased availability of game titles in the market could also lead to increased competition and lower consumer prices, which may result in reduced revenue per item and fewer item sales, ultimately impacting revenue negatively. Profit should be impacted negatively if AI adoption is done at a slower pace than the market average. The effect could be counterbalanced if large publishers adopt AI aggressively, thereby lowering their service costs and remaining relevant to developers who require their services. The lower cost of production would also negate the potential lower revenue pressure stemming from lower item prices, which could reduce the revenue per item and profitability.

"This is still early days. Right now, I suspect these tools are having a negative effect on productivity. But that's part of the investment. People are learning, building muscle. They know the tools will improve. They know they'll be outpaced if they don't adapt. So they're putting in the time."

—Interview with Stephen Peacock
Director AI at 2K, Ex-Head of AI at AWS & Keywords

*"Il va y avoir une rapide montée de retour sur investissement lorsque les gens vont comprendre comment utiliser l'IA de manière efficace. [...]
Nous pourrons créer des jeux de niveau AAA en 6 mois avec 4 personnes, au lieu du présent 1500+ personnes pendant 7 ans."*

AI translation: "There's going to be a rapid rise in ROI as people figure out how to use AI effectively. [...] We'll be able to create AAA-level games in 6 months with 4 people, instead of the present 1500+ people for 7 years."

—Interview with Stéphanie Bouchard
Freelance Game Designer/Director - Oxitocyn
Ex Leadership & AI positions at Stockholm Syndrome.AI, Red Barrels, WBGM, Ubisoft, THQ
Ex Game Teacher at NAD-UQAC, Campus ADN, Champlain College, Dawson College
Research contributor at MIT and Concordia University

Higher focus on User Generated Content (UGC)

AI will democratize game creation further, the same way that game engines did. Creating games will become increasingly easy, and creating content for and from gamers is expected to increase also in an important fashion. We can expect an increase in business models that focus on user-generated content (UGC) rather than company-built content. Harnessing the power of millions, if not billions, of gamers to create value is more effective than using hundreds/thousands of developers. Social web rose in popularity and value because of Web 2.0 principles of rich user experiences, architectures of participation, and harnessing collective intelligence.[110] The same will be true with some disrupting game companies. Although still not profitable yet, Roblox is an example of that. This shift will affect and potentially disrupt many B2C and B2B game companies that rely on more traditional business models.

---

[110] Implications of connectivity and accessibility, Minnalearn, https://courses.minnalearn.com/en/courses/digital-revolution/the-internet-and-connectivity-revolution/the-implications-of-connectivity-and-accessibility/, visited 7 October 2024

> *"Notre business model va changer. L'IA va ouvrir les portes au contenu généré par les joueurs, par des joueurs qui interagissent et changent le jeu de façon plus drastique. Le modding va devenir très populaire."*
>
> *AI translation: "Our business model will change. AI will open the door to more player-generated content, allowing players to interact and change the game more drastically. Modding is going to become very popular."*
>
> —Interview with Stéphanie Bouchard
> Freelance Game Designer/Director - Oxitocyn
> Ex Leadership & AI positions at Stockholm Syndrome.AI, Red Barrels, WBGM, Ubisoft, THQ
> Ex Game Teacher at NAD-UQAC, Campus ADN, Champlain College, Dawson College
> Research contributor at MIT and Concordia University

> *"Jusqu'à présent, on ne croyait pas particulièrement au UGC (User Generated Content). Mais je pense que c'est aussi un truc qui va bouleverser beaucoup de choses. [...] Je crois que les UGCs, surtout avec l'industrie du jeu vidéo en temps de crise, pourrait être une des réponses."*
>
> *AI translation: "Until now, we didn't particularly believe in UGC (User Generated Content). But I think it's also something that's going to change a lot of things. [...] I think UGCs, especially with the video game industry in a time of crisis, could be one of the answers."*
>
> —Interview with Félix Balmonet
> Co-Founder & CEO, Chat3D

Gaming subindustries to be disrupted

Despite the current lag in AI adoption for game development, we can expect most game service niches or specialties to be disrupted at some point due to their high occupational workload exposure to AI automation.

In most cases, it seems like the biggest tipping point for each is ease of use and awareness by its target audience. A lot of the AI tools that could generate cost efficiencies or productivity gains already exist. As of October 7, 2024, Hugging Face, a popular AI repository, lists over 1,036,000 AI models, 261,000 AI applications, and 222,000 datasets for AI and ML use. Some notable organizations contributing to and leveraging these models include Meta, Microsoft, Google, Amazon, Sony, Runway, Stability AI, Nvidia,

Intel, AMD, and IBM. While the repository and its content are not general-public, user-friendly themselves, many of the more popular public-use AI tools can and do leverage this content. Think of it as front-end vs. back-end. A lot of the back-end already exists, but the general public isn't leveraging it because there is no user-friendly front-end that currently allows them to do so. Once someone builds a user-friendly front-end, a tipping point often appears. [111]

Many of the AI tools we've explored are either disrupting the industry already or are likely to do so soon.

> *"Il va y avoir de l'économie pour les studios. Ça va coûter moins cher aux studios. Ça se peut que ça se résulte de la même façon quand les chaînes de production ont été automatisées il y a quelques dizaines d'années. Ça demande une transformation du travail. Mais ça va se faire au bénéfice de la qualité. Les jeux qui vont se démarquer vont être de meilleure qualité."*
>
> *AI translation: "There will be savings for the studios. It's going to cost the studios less. It may turn out the same way as when production lines were automated a few decades ago. It requires a transformation of work. But it's going to be to the benefit of quality. The games that stand out are going to be of better quality."*
>
> —Interview with Pierre-Paul Giroux
> Vice-President Engineering A.I. at Unity

Game Design: 90%+ of game design can currently be automated via AI. Even 95%+ for concept art.

For most of the game design steps, while I do believe that there will be some work displacement, and there already is, I don't believe that it will reach such high numbers. I believe that more and better content will come from the pre-existing teams. Game companies always need more and better ideas, more and better game concepts, better-written scripts, and better documentation to help increase and improve the output and alignment from their teams. The companies that leverage AI to create more and better content will force all of their competitors to do the same by increasing the quality bar for all.

For concept art specifically, there has been a rapidly growing movement in the last couple of years, where the position of concept artist is either replaced by AI specialists or at least augmented by concept artists using AI to generate images. There are an increasing number of producers using AI image generators themselves. They bypass previously used artists, contractors, and whole departments to be able to "fail fast" and create in mere seconds what used to take weeks of work to create. [112]

---

[111] Hugging Face, https://huggingface.co/huggingface, visited 7 October 2024

[112] AI is replacing artists, and here's the proof, Paul Hatton, Creative Bloq, https://www.creativebloq.com/news/ai-is-taking-artists-jobs, 6 October 2023

Game Engineering: While relatively stable for now, and only partially influenced by the use of AI code review and supplementation, the release of OpenAI's o1 and the expectation of newer releases to come from OpenAI and others will likely soon have more impact on the productivity of engineering teams. While the field is obviously expected to change, it is unknown if the high level of automation potential will reduce work demands or not, industry-wide. We believe it will likely remain somewhat stable, as any work that can be automated is compensated for by generating more content for larger and more extensive games, which this technology would enable. Some of the larger tasks for game engineers are the implementation and coordination of all assets. If AI generates more content to implement, then more implementation efforts may be needed.

Visual Art Creation: Within the span of a few years, AI tools brought game visual art creation automation capabilities from nil to almost 70% of assets. This field has one of the largest amounts of current and upcoming AI players, and we've seen drastic improvements this year alone, including Midjourney, DALL-E, Sora, and others. Tools like Meshy and Genie include increasingly accurate AI model creation and rendering. Tools like Audio2Face and AccuRIG are also increasingly reducing the amount of time that animators historically spent on manual work. While the field is obviously expected to change, it is unknown if the high level of AI automation potential will reduce work demands or not, industry-wide. While we believe that demand will reduce temporarily, it will likely stabilize and then increase as the quality and quantity bar increases via AI automation. more and bigger games will compensate for the efficiency gain.

Audio Creation: Within a few years, AI tools have brought automation capabilities for game audio creation from nil to over 85% of assets. The field is improving rapidly, with the current market leader, ElevenLabs, and new competitors continually addressing untapped niches. Classic recording studios and pipelines are likely to experience diminished demand for their services, not just in gaming, but also from traditional entertainment sectors such as TV, movies, and music. On one hand, this field is poised to be disrupted in a significant way. On the other hand, the lower production costs brought about by AI will also enable more and better audio in games. For example, many games don't currently feature voiceovers. The lower production costs may allow adding VOs to most games easily from now on.

Quality Assurance: QA appears to be temporarily shielded from AI, or at least further removed from many other specialities, primarily due to the complexity of some tasks and the variance in required tasks from one title to another. The easier and more repetitive tasks, like compliance/certification testing checklists for first-party publishers like Sony, Microsoft, and Nintendo, are likely to be automated first. However, many QA tasks require AI bots, which are either costly to create and customize, or AI agents, for which the technology is still in its infancy.

Additionally, the volume of content to be tested determines the demand for QA's work. With AI making it easier to create more content, demand for the service could increase, compensating for what can be automated via AI. For example, if organisations leverage AI to create games that are 10 times larger or have 10 times more content, QA needs may increase where automation, via AI or otherwise, isn't possible. Note that this effect may be temporary only, though, until technology catches up with what we'd like it to do.

Localization: Should the linear progression of machine translation explored previously continue steadily, we should expect machine translation quality to be on par with human translators' before 2030, and even require no human-in-the-loop before 2040. By then, AI would outperform the vast majority of human translators at a cost so low that it could be offered sustainably free by many various AI platforms. This is true not only of games' localization, but for most of the localization industry. Regarding voiceovers, if leveraged, current AI technology is likely able to replace nearly 90% of game-level quality content. In both of these cases, we should not only expect cost efficiency but also an increase in content output. This would mean more games being localized in more languages, as the cost barrier diminishes, and as ROI increases for new markets and languages for games to be localized into.

As per the previous QA example, this could mean an increased need and demand in Localization QA, as more content needs to be verified. Again, note that this effect may be temporary only, until technology catches up on what we'd like it to do.

> *"I think that will also create some interesting competitive behavior in the third-party developers developing these solutions because they will be trying to develop something that can be bundled or plugged in easily to the commercial engines. I think that will really spur on the development. There'll be a lot of competition there because whoever wins will win in that space, whether it's having their tech acquired by Epic and rolled out as part of the Unreal Engine, or everyone just adopting it as the de facto plug-in when they're working on Unreal Engine games, for example."*
>
> —Interview with Jamie Campbell
> Founder of MTX Solutions, Co-Founder of d3t Studio, ex-ATI (AMD), ex-Technical Director at THQ

Non-AI-supported B2B Games services outsourcing organizations to be disrupted

B2B games outsourcing organizations provide the gaming subindustry services described previously. As such, as developers and publishers are able to manage their work volume more easily overflows themselves by leveraging AI, their need to outsource may diminish. One exception arises, though, which has been and will remain a constant in the field: if B2B outsourcers continue to find ways to be less expensive than the developer or publisher doing the work themselves, due to AI or otherwise, the need and demand for outsourcing will persist. It thus becomes imperative for those B2B outsourcers to aggressively focus on AI/automation and other cost-reduction plans to keep up with demand and stay relevant. This is even more true in the short term, as the industry is facing significant budget cuts and layoffs, and company executives are seeking ways to reduce costs.

The context is even more relevant for individual contractors and small businesses, which are often more prone to market fluctuations. We should expect many gaming "mom-and-pop" shops to close down in the upcoming few years, with some of the more well-known ones in subindustry niches being acquired by larger companies.

The size of the market could potentially be reduced temporarily. Some market consolidation, through business closures and M&A, should occur, especially for the businesses that won't be able to adapt to these new market and technological realities.

> *"I am one 100% confident that there will absolutely be transformative AI technologies to game development. [...] But, because the teams won't move fast enough to adopt these technologies, some of the people making these technologies will go out of business. Just because it's a good business case doesn't mean anybody adopts it."*
>
> -Interview with Matt Ditton
> CEO and Co-Founder of Mighty Games Group & Mighty Build and Test

AI implementation service employees and organizations to appear and grow drastically

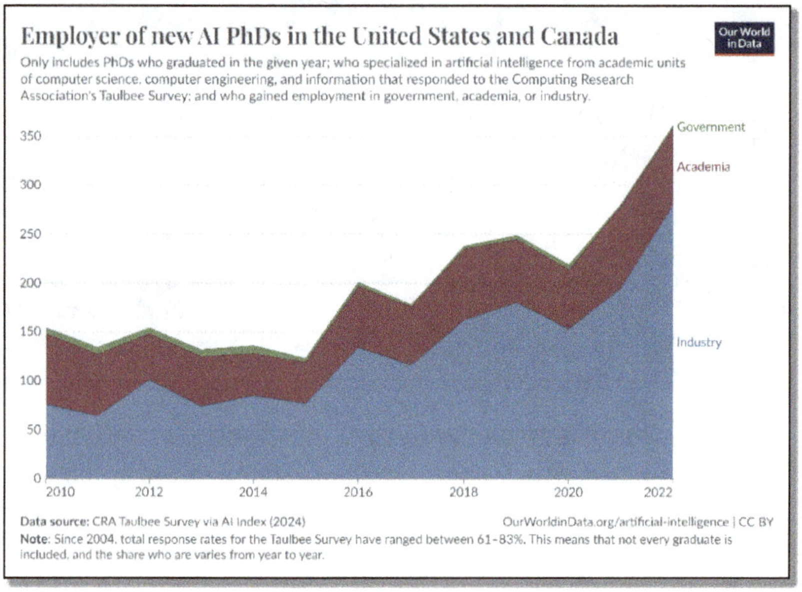

As described previously, there is a wide disparity between what AI can currently do and what it currently does in organizations, in the gaming industry and out. Currently, AI capabilities are immense but not being fully leveraged. Most of it is due to a knowledge gap and resistance to change. As such, we should expect an important increase in the number and size of players offering AI implementation and consulting services to organizations. There will likely be a gold rush for AI-related consulting organizations. On the right, visual data representing the number of newly employed AI PhDs in the United States and Canada (2010-2022).[113]

[113] Employer of new AI PhDs in the United States and Canada, Our World in Data, https://ourworldindata.org/grapher/employer-new-artificial-intelligence-phds-stacked-area, 28 June 2024

"Whether it's companies investing in AI training or individuals exploring tools on their own, the time spent comes with a productivity cost. That cost is real, even if the upskilling payoff will come later."

-Interview with Stephen Peacock
Director AI at 2K, Ex-Head of AI at AWS & Keywords

AI training and MOOC demand to grow exponentially, and niche competitors to appear

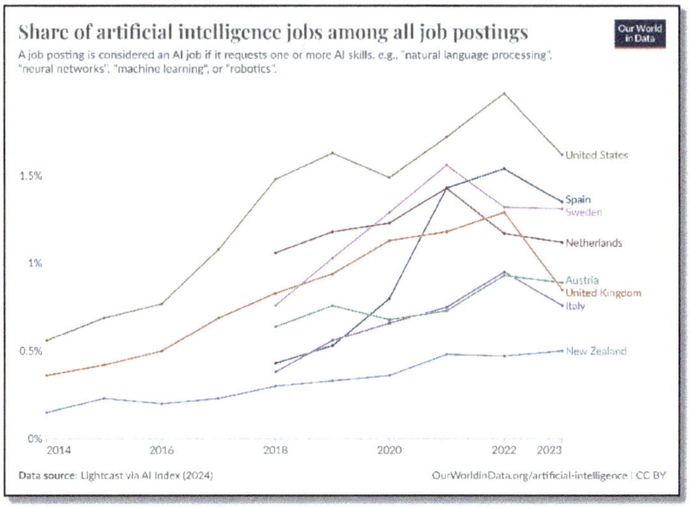

Universities and online training platforms are scrambling to meet the current demand for AI courses, specializations, and degrees. People and organizations are trying to upskill themselves as rapidly as possible. The demand is expected to grow even further. In 2023, on average, Coursera added 1 new AI course user every minute. Nine months into 2024, that number has now jumped to 6 per minute. As of January 2024, they already have over 800 AI-related courses. This increased demand will also likely mean increased competition from new providers offering additional generic and niche AI trainings.[114,115,116]

[114] ChatGPT effect: Coursera sees signups for AI courses every minute in 2023, Divya Chowdhury et al., https://www.reuters.com/technology/chatgpt-effect-coursera-sees-signups-ai-courses-every-minute-2023-2024-01-18/, 18 January 2024

[115] Coursera Inc (COUR) Q3 2024 Earnings Call Highlights: Solid Growth Amidst Challenges, GuruFocus News, yahoo!finance, https://finance.yahoo.com/news/coursera-inc-cour-q3-2024-072102889.html, 25 October 2024

[116] Share of artificial intelligence jobs among all job postings, Lightcast via AI Index, Our World in Data, https://ourworldindata.org/grapher/share-artificial-intelligence-job-postings, 8 June 2024

"Il ne faut pas s'imaginer que les startups qui sont là actuellement seront encore là dans 30 ans. Je pense même que les plus gros acteurs qui vont réussir à se conserver, ce sera de l'intégration dans un produit. Je pense qu'il faut vraiment avoir une vision de produit plutôt qu'une vision de technologie, Je pense que les fonctionnalités de produits survivront, mais pas les entreprises."

AI translation: "We shouldn't imagine that the startups that are here now will still be there in 30 years' time. I think that the biggest players who will manage to hold on to their position will be product integrators. I think you really need to have a product vision rather than a technology vision, I think product functionality will survive, but companies won't."

—Interview with Félix Balmonet
Co-Founder & CEO, Chat3D

"There seem to have been so few commercial winners to date. A lot of the time I was thinking, it's going to be horrible one of these days when we don't make a move on one of these companies or we don't make a small investment. And then we see them, off to the moon and hitting the hockey stick and we've missed out. But I don't think that's happened once. And I struggle to think who are the big winners at the moment apart from the Open AIs of the world. And they're winning the race, but they're not winning the commercial side of things."

—Interview with Jamie Campbell
Founder of MTX Solutions, Co-Founder of d3t Studio, ex-ATI (AMD), ex-Technical Director at THQ

AI tool organizations to appear and grow drastically, but also falter

New and better AI tools are coming out every week, but because organizational implementation is lagging, we believe that it's not currently driven by market demand, but by the high number and amount of investments in the sector. If that's the case and adoption doesn't pick up drastically, we believe that the full ecosystem won't be sustainable, both in gaming and beyond. The AI industry is growing aggressively, with various analysts expecting a compound annual growth rate (CAGR) between 19% and 42% by 2030, and most proposing numbers varying between 30% and 35%. There is currently a limited market size for all potential players and newcomers. As such, we should expect some type of market consolidation through AI business closures and mergers and acquisitions (M&A).

> *"There will be lots of disruption. You'll instantly get other people coming in with startups to build on the shoulders of giants that went before them and died, because that kind of foundation that's been built is never going to go away, and they'll try and fix the legal and ethical problems that were there. It's still a starting point to progress to the next level of sophistication. I can see this really high cadence of startup fold startup fold startup fold, and it's when you reach that critical mass where the adoption takes place. Some people will win, but I think that there'll be a lot more losers than winners."*
>
> —Interview with Jamie Campbell
> Founder of MTX Solutions, Co-Founder of d3t Studio, ex-ATI (AMD), ex-Technical Director at THQ

Additionally, there is a significant gap between the low prices of many AI tools and the high value they deliver. This could yield a few outcomes. First, if it fits their strategy, tool providers could raise prices and boost profits. This could help negate the effect raised previously. Second, new players may be enticed to enter the market if they're very profitable. This could potentially destabilize the AI market even further, but also increase tool options and efficiency for clients. [117,118,119,120]

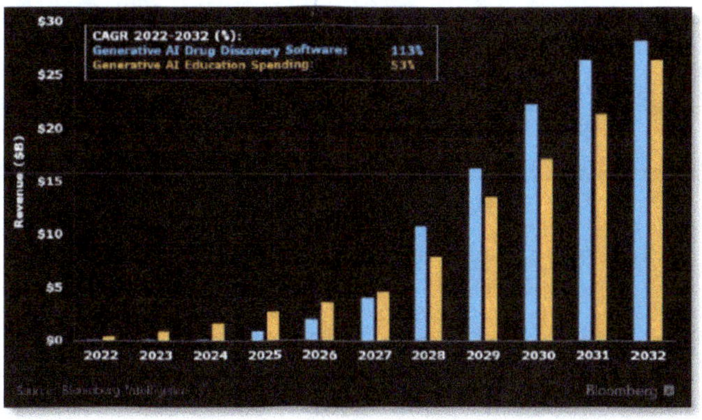

[117] Global Artificial Intelligence Market Size (2024-2033), Market.us, https://market.us/report/artificial-intelligence-market/, September 2024

[118] The global AI market is expected to reach $1.81 trillion by 2030, Faist, https://www.faistgroup.com/news/global-ai-market-2030/, 11 June 2024

[119] Generative AI to Become a $1.3 Trillion Market by 2032, Research Finds, Mandeep Singh et al., Bloomberg, https://www.bloomberg.com/company/press/generative-ai-to-become-a-1-3-trillion-market-by-2032-research-finds/, 1 June 2024

[120] Global Artificial Intelligence (AI) Market: Investments vs Potential, BCC Publishing, https://www.bccresearch.com/market-research/information-technology/artificial-intelligence-market-report.html, August 2024

"When talking to people involved in doing this work, we've consistently seen that there is excitement and leaning into the notion of not having to do the repetitive tasks. [...] You could make the straw man argument that automation and AI will take our jobs, but in reality, all the people that we've talked to have been very much for it."

—Interview with Christoffer Holmgård
CEO and Co-Founder of modl.ai

"Mon take sur le marché est un peu bleak, et je ne suis pas une personne bleak. [...] Faire ça (l'IA), ça coûte extrêmement cher. Puis à un moment donné, il n'y aura plus d'argent pour ça. [...] J'ai l'impression que la bulle va péter, la bulle des Pure AI Companies. Mais vu que la tech va déjà exister, après ça, les vrais applications vont exploser la quantité de choses que les gens peuvent faire."

AI translation: "My take on the market is a bit bleak, and I'm not a bleak person. [...] It's extremely expensive to do that (AI). At some point, there won't be any money left for it. [...] I have a feeling that the Pure AI companies bubble is going to burst. But since the tech will exist at that point, the amount of things that people will be able to do with AI will explode."

—Interview with Pierre-Paul Giroux
Vice-President Engineering A.I. at Unity

"At conferences, a lot of people are saying the same thing they said last year. That this year was all about prototypes, and next year will be the year we actually ship real work. Investors want to believe that story, because many of these AI startups aren't seeing traction. You can sense the desperation. Some of these companies are flickering in and out of existence."

—Interview with Stephen Peacock
Director AI at 2K, Ex-Head of AI at AWS & Keywords

"[Referencing Gartner's AI hype curve] There's an analogy with the Amazon business case. A lot of the internet companies died during the internet bubble crash, but a lot of positive and success came out of it, like Amazon. [...] Chances are, not all of those AI companies will survive. [...] There's a lot of stuff that we do that no one cares about, but they should. My job is to stay alive long enough for everyone to catch up to us. To realize that they need this. That they need us."

—Interview with Matt Ditton
CEO and Co-Founder of Mighty Games Group & Mighty Build and Test

As AI adoption progresses, some traditional jobs will disappear, and their salaries will go down

As mentioned, AI can be applied to many traditional gaming jobs. Although these technological changes will bring a multitude of new roles and opportunities, there is a high chance that they will also reduce the demand for human work in some more traditional roles affected by AI automation. This is likely to lead to lower demand, fewer hires, more layoffs, and lower salaries in those fields, at least for a time. While we're not exploring job displacement and retraining in this research, it is a reality in the game industry that most companies and employees must address and prepare for, sooner rather than later.

AI adoption will impact workforce dynamics and role transformations. It will very likely generate long-term effects on development processes, team structures, and industry standards. It will generate new opportunities, but also present new challenges within existing workflows, training requirements, and potential resistance to change among development teams.

*"I think that I can see two bubbles of how to look at AI. Like [*Redacted large game publisher name*]. They are saying they're using AI. But when they say they're using AI, it feels a bit dirty. It's just automating jobs away wherever possible. But I think [*they*] had this negative underlying tone the entire time. And then, for indie game developers, I see a lot of people who make no money, they're really passionate, and they just want to make stuff. And now they can make stuff more easily. I think the way AI is approached in these two groups is very different."*

—Interview with Dylan Ebert, PhD
Developer Advocate Engineer, Hugging Face

"You'd hope to think that that wouldn't mean less resources making games. You'd hope it would mean richer games with more content and higher quality."

—Interview with Jamie Campbell
Founder of MTX Solutions, Co-Founder of d3t Studio, ex-ATI (AMD), ex-Technical Director at THQ

8 LIMITATIONS

The following sections outline the limitations of this study I could determine, both in terms of the research methodology and the broader field of AI in game development. These limitations provide context for interpreting the results and highlight areas for future research.

8.1 RESEARCH LIMITATIONS

This study faced some limitations which may have affected the findings and their interpretation. Although it took a comprehensive approach, certain constraints are inherent to the research process.

First, the focus was primarily on quantifiable metrics, like cost efficiency and productivity gains. This doesn't fully capture the broader impact of elements such as speed/time/turnaround, quality improvements, resource utilization, and risk management. Also, I reviewed each gaming field along with its potential AI impacts individually, treating them as standalone entities. This doesn't consider how different fields might influence one another. Additionally, the expert interviews involved a limited number of professionals. A larger and more diverse sample could have offered a wider range of insights and perspectives.

The rapid advancement of AI technology also poses a challenge; some tools or techniques have changed during the research period, which would affect the relevance of certain findings. As mentioned in the preface, the AI tools evaluated in this research were assessed based on their capabilities and performance as of the end of 2024. Newer tools and updates are not included in this analysis. The expectation is that, as time goes by, the cost efficiency and productivity potential of AI applications would grow even further.

Finally, the self-examination and experimentation phase, while beneficial, may be influenced by my personal bias and lacks the scope of larger industry implementations. These limitations should be taken into account when interpreting the results of this study.

> *"I don't have concerns about AI reducing the quality of games. Games are already bad. You don't need AI to make bad games. People are doing fine on their own."*
>
> —Interview with Matt Ditton
>
> CEO and Co-Founder of Mighty Games Group & Mighty Build and Test

"Une IA peut produire quelque chose de beau. Mais sans parcours, sans émotion, sans incertitudes créatives et donc sans intention humaine derrière, ce n'est pas une œuvre. L'art ne vient pas du rendu, mais de ce que l'on cherche à faire ressentir."

AI translation: "AI can produce something beautiful. But without a journey, without emotion, without creative uncertainties, and therefore without human intention behind it, it is not a work of art. Art does not come from the rendering, but from what we seek to convey."

—Interview with Frederic Vicaire
Founder and Creative Director of art!equin agency

Field limitations

While this study provides valuable insights into AI in game development, some broader limitations in the field may affect our comprehensive understanding and application of these technologies.

The potential impact of AI adoption on workforce dynamics, including possible job displacement, role transformations, and union responses, requires further examination. Given the nascent stage of many AI applications in game development, the long-term effects on development processes, team structures, and industry standards remain unclear. Additionally, while this study measured productivity and cost efficiency, it did not extensively assess AI's influence on creative aspects, such as game design innovation and artistic expression.

"What's going to be more interesting for the game industry is if they can figure out how they use AI to make game experiences that they weren't able to do before. We haven't had something really disrupt the game industry since mobile. Can AI do something that is completely ingenious? Something never possible before? It will be interesting to see the first studios to give us something new and novel into game experiences."

—Interview with Liza Wood
Principal Group Program Manager – Data & AI Leader at Microsoft
Ex-Disney/WB Games/Behavior/EA

Practical challenges in implementing AI solutions, such as integration with existing workflows, training requirements, and potential resistance to change within development teams, were not addressed. The legal and ethical implications of AI use in game development, including copyright issues with AI-generated content and ethical concerns in the creative process, were also not explored.

These field-specific limitations underscore the need for ongoing research and exploration to fully comprehend the multifaceted impact of AI on the game development industry.

> *"I think there's always the undertone of risk, legal, ethical, and reputational risk of adopting Gen AI, not just in kind of runtime in games, but also in the development processes of games. So I think that we would want some safeguards around that."*
>
> —Interview with Jamie Campbell
> Founder of MTX Solutions, Co-Founder of d3t Studio, ex-ATI (AMD), ex-Technical Director at THQ

> *"There are a lot of things to think about. There are privacy concerns, there are technology costs. I think the world has demonstrated it doesn't care too much about privacy. And technology costs a lot of money until eventually it doesn't."*
>
> —Interview with Matt Ditton
> CEO and Co-Founder of Mighty Games Group & Mighty Build and Test

“On a accidentellement fait un IA suicidaire. […] On met des poids tentatifs dans les récompenses et les punitions de l’agent. On le laisse rouler durant la nuit. Le lendemain matin, l’agent tente de se mettre devant un ennemi et attend de se faire tirer. […] Tout faisait tellement mal que la meilleure option, c'était d'arrêter de souffrir immédiatement.”

AI translation: "We accidentally made a suicidal AI. [...] We put tentative weights on the agent's rewards and punishments, and let him run through the night. By the next morning, the agent was getting right in front of enemies, waiting to get shot. [...] Everything hurt so much that the best option for it was to stop suffering immediately."

—Interview with Stéphanie Bouchard
Freelance Game Designer/Director - Oxitocyn
Ex Leadership & AI positions at Stockholm Syndrome.AI, Red Barrels, WBGM, Ubisoft, THQ
Ex Game Teacher at NAD-UQAC, Campus ADN, Champlain College, Dawson College
Research contributor at MIT and Concordia University

9 REFERENCES

1. GPT-4 Technical Report, OpenAI, https://cdn.openai.com/papers/gpt-4.pdf, 27 March 2023
2. Learning to Reason with LLMs, OpenAI, https://openai.com/index/learning-to-reason-with-llms/, 12 September 2024
3. Generative AI could raise global GDP by 7%, Goldman Sachs, https://www.goldmansachs.com/intelligence/pages/generative-ai-could-raise-global-gdp-by-7-percent.html, 5 April 2023
4. 2023–2024 video game industry layoffs, Wikipedia, https://en.wikipedia.org/wiki/2023%E2%80%932024_video_game_industry_layoffs, visited 14 July 2024
5. GDC State of the Game Industry 2023 report, GDC, https://reg.gdconf.com/state-of-game-industry-2024, January 2024
6. Market insights Video Games – Worldwide, Statista, https://www.statista.com/outlook/dmo/digital-media/video-games/worldwide, March 2024
7. Create hit games with the power of AI, Ludo.ai, https://ludo.ai/, visited July 2024
8. Gemini API Pricing, Google, https://ai.google.dev/pricing, 31 July 2024
9. Pricing, OpenAI, https://openai.com/api/pricing/, 29 July 2024
10. A guide to concept art estimation, M. Goodarzi, https://pixune.com/blog/concept-art-price/, 11 July 2024
11. Training & Datasets, Leonardo.ai, https://app.leonardo.ai/training-datasets, July 2024
12. Perplexity – Enterprise Pro, Perplexity, https://www.perplexity.ai/enterprise, August 2024
13. The Convergence of AI and Creativity: Introducing Ghostwriter, R. Barth, Ubisoft, https://news.ubisoft.com/en-us/article/7Cm07zbBGy4Xml6WgYi25d/the-convergence-of-ai-and-creativity-introducing-ghostwriter, 21 March 2023
14. About billing for GitHub Copilot Individual, GitHub Docs, https://docs.github.com/en/copilot/managing-copilot/managing-copilot-as-an-individual-subscriber/managing-your-copilot-subscription/about-billing-for-github-copilot-individual, October 2024
15. How good is enough? AI vs. human code, SAP LeanIX, https://engineering.leanix.net/blog/ai-vs-human-code/, 16 Dec 2022
16. Project AVA: Game development with AI, Keywords Studios, GDC 2004, https://www.keywordsstudios.com/en/ava-at-gdc/, April 2024
17. Productivity Assessment of Neural Code Completion, GitHub team, https://dl.acm.org/doi/pdf/10.1145/3520312.3534864, 12 June 2022
18. Scientifically Measuring the True Impact of Generative AI Software Development, A. Girzhadovich, Exadel, https://exadel.com/news/measuring-generative-ai-software-development/, 14 May 2024
19. What is ChatGPT?, OpenAI, https://help.openai.com/en/articles/6783457-what-is-chatgpt, August 2024
20. Will humans even write code in 2040 and what would that mean for extreme heterogeneity in computing?, Oak Ridge National Laboratory, https://arxiv.org/pdf/1712.00676, 19 Dec 2017
21. Research: quantifying GitHub Copilot's impact on developer productivity and happiness, GitHub, https://github.blog/news-insights/research/research-quantifying-github-copilots-impact-on-developer-productivity-and-happiness/, 21 May 2024

22. Is GitHub Copilot Worth It? Real-World Data Reveals the Answer, Faros.ai, https://www.faros.ai/blog/is-github-copilot-worth-it-real-world-data-reveals-the-answer, 17 May 2024
23. Coding on Copilot, GitClear, https://gitclear-public.s3.us-west-2.amazonaws.com/Coding-on-Copilot-2024-Developer-Research.pdf, 16 Jan 2024
24. AI for Game Development: How Code Maestro is Making Waves, iLOGOS, https://ilogos.biz/ai-for-game-development-how-code-maestro-is-making-waves/, 15 May 2024
25. AI vs Crunch Time: How to Save 50% of Game Development Time with Code Maestro, Alexander Goldybin, Code Maestro, https://www.youtube.com/watch?v=U8k5jvZvDgo, 20 June 2024
26. Buildbox AI, https://signup.buildbox.com/, visited 1 August 2024
27. Game Programmer Vs Software Engineer, Zippia, https://www.zippia.com/game-programmer-jobs/game-programmer-vs-software-engineer-differences/, 5 April 2024
28. Learning to Reason with LLMs: Coding, OpenAI, https://openai.com/index/learning-to-reason-with-llms/, 12 September 2024
29. The Art of Game Design: A book of lenses, Jesse Schell, August 2008
30. How the Use of AI Evolved Our Art Production Pipelines, Mario Toon, Mighty Bear Games, https://www.mightybeargames.com/post/how-the-use-of-ai-evolved-our-art-production-pipelines, 25 October 2023
31. Creating an AI-Assisted Art Tool to Optimize Efficiency in Game Art, Quinnie Cheuk, Medium, https://medium.com/mighty-bear-games/creating-an-ai-assisted-art-tool-to-optimize-efficiency-in-game-art-bf2a7c5e53ef, 2 August 2023
32. How Much Does it Cost to Create 3D Models?, Amélie Deltombe, https://sketchfab.com/blogs/enterprise/create-3d-models-cost, 20 October 2020
33. A Guide to 2D Art & 3D Art Outsourcing Costs and Value, Pixune, https://pixune.com/blog/game-art-outsourcing-price/, 22 August 2024
34. Meshy.AI, https://www.meshy.ai/, visited July 2024
35. Genie, Luma Labs, https://lumalabs.ai/genie, visited July 2024
36. Luma API, Luma Labs, https://lumalabs.ai/luma-api, visited July 2024
37. About Us, Kaedim, https://www.kaedim3d.com/about-us, visited July 2024
38. Case Studies, Kaedim, https://www.kaedim3d.com/case-study, visited July 2024
39. How much does a character design cost? How to choose the right character design company, Juego Studios, https://www.juegostudio.com/blog/character-design-cost, 19 June 2023
40. AccuRIG, Actorcore (Reallusion), https://actorcore.reallusion.com/auto-rig/accurig, visited July 2024
41. 3D Animation and Automated Rigging, Anything World, https://anything.world/, visited July 2024
42. Muse, Unity, https://unity.com/products/muse, visited August 2024
43. Promethean AI, https://www.prometheanai.com/, visited July 2024
44. AI World Building, Promethean AI, https://www.prometheanai.com/ai-world-building, visited July 2024
45. AI asset management, Promethean AI, https://www.prometheanai.com/asset-management, visited July 2024

46. Magnific AI – The magic image upscaler & enhancer, Magnific AI, https://magnific.ai/#games, visited August 2024
47. Unity New AI Tools Review - Muse Animate, Chat, Texture, Behavior and Sprite - Are They Any Good?, GameFromScratch, https://gamefromscratch.com/unity-ai-muse-tools-review/, 25 April 2024
48. 2D skeletons, Godot, https://docs.godotengine.org/en/stable/tutorials/animation/2d_skeletons.html, 2014
49. Creature: The Automated animation Tool, Kestrel Moon, https://www.kestrelmoon.com/creature/more_info_2.html, visited August 2024
50. Animated Drawings, Meta, https://sketch.metademolab.com/, visited July 2024
51. 2D sprite animation, Godot Engine 4.3 Documentation, Godot, https://docs.godotengine.org/en/stable/tutorials/2d/2d_sprite_animation.html, visited August 2024
52. 3D VFX Cost + Influencing Factors, Nazanin Shahbazi, https://pixune.com/blog/3d-vfx-cost/, 22 August 2024
53. Generative VFX with Runway Gen-3 | Create AI Visual Effects, Kevin Hutson, Futurepedia, https://www.youtube.com/watch?v=pGEW7AKcLrg, 19 August 2024
54. How Much Does It Cost To Make A Cinematic Trailer?, Animost Team, https://animost.com/uncategorized/how-much-does-it-cost-to-make-a-cinematic-trailer/,8 November 2023
55. 3D Animation Costs in 2024: Rates and Budget Management Tips, Rocket Brush Studio, https://rocketbrush.com/blog/how-much-does-3d-animation-cost-per-minute-in-2024-rates-and-budget-management-tips, 27 March 2024
56. Video generation models as world simulators, OpenAI, https://openai.com/index/video-generation-models-as-world-simulators/, 15 February 2024
57. VideoFX, Google's AI Test Kitchen, https://aitestkitchen.withgoogle.com/tools/video-fx, visited August 2024
58. How Video Is Failing To Enhance And Promote Games, Barry Jenkins, Forbes, https://www.forbes.com/councils/forbestechcouncil/2021/09/17/how-video-is-failing-to-enhance-and-promote-games/, 17 September 2021
59. How much do video game sound effects cost? A comprehensive guide, ElevenLabs, https://elevenlabs.io/blog/how-much-do-video-game-sound-effects-cost, 9 April 2024
60. Budget for sound design in video games, Mikhail Repin, https://repinsound.com/tpost/9o29zahie1-budget-for-sound-design-in-video-games, 4 May 2023
61. How to incorporate AI sound effect generators in your game development process, ElevenLabs, https://elevenlabs.io/blog/ai-sound-effect-generators-in-games, 10 April 2024
62. Understanding how much a game music project costs, Flutu, https://flutumusic.com/understanding-how-much-a-game-music-project-costs/, visited September 2024
63. Budgeting for Audio in Your Game's Crowdfunding Campaign, Kole Hicks, Game Developer, https://www.gamedeveloper.com/audio/budgeting-for-audio-in-your-game-s-crowdfunding-campaign, 23 May 2016
64. Suno, https://suno.com/, visited September 2024

65. Udio beta, https://www.udio.com/, visited September 2024
66. What to Charge as a Voiceover Artist, Backstage, https://www.backstage.com/magazine/article/voiceover-artist-rate-guide-834/, 22 February 2024
67. A VO's Journey Voice Over Rate Guide, Anthony Pica, https://www.avosjourney.com/voice-over-rate-guide, visited September 2024
68. Paradox Interactive speeds up audio generation from weeks to hours with ElevenLabs, ElevenLabs, https://elevenlabs.io/blog/paradox-interactive, 30 June 2023
69. Creating realistic AI generated character voices for games, ElevenLabs, https://elevenlabs.io/blog/ai-generated-character-voices-for-games, 21 June 2024
70. AMGI and ElevenLabs partnership, AMGI Studios, https://x.com/amgistudios/status/1811786492542415318, 12 July 2024
71. Cumulative distribution function, Wikipedia, https://en.wikipedia.org/wiki/Cumulative_distribution_function, visited June 2024
72. Three Must-Ask Questions about the Cost of Localizing a Game, LangLink, https://langlinking.com/three-must-ask-questions-about-the-cost-of-localizing-a-game/, 26 July 2022
73. Breaking Down the Cost of Game Localization, Naarg, https://www.naargmedia.com/cost-of-game-localization/, visited July 2024
74. Demystifying Game Localization Costs: A Comprehensive Guide, Transphere, https://www.transphere.com/game-localization-costs/, 25 April 2024
75. The 3 main factors to calculate the game localization cost in 2023!, Sherif Abuizd, https://translationpartner.com/game-localization-cost/, visited July 2024
76. BLEU: a Method for Automatic Evaluation of Machine Translation, Kishore Papineni et al., Proceedings of the 40th Annual Meeting of the Association for Computational Linguistics (ACL), https://aclanthology.org/P02-1040.pdf, July 2002
77. Findings of the 2019 Conference on Machine Translation (WMT19), Proceedings of the Fourth Conference on Machine Translation (WMT), https://aclanthology.org/W19-5301.pdf, August 2019
78. This Is the Speed at Which We Are Approaching Singularity in AI, Translated, https://translated.com/speed-to-singularity, visited June 2024
79. Cramming more components onto integrated circuits, Moore, Gordon E., Stanford, http://cva.stanford.edu/classes/cs99s/papers/moore-crammingmorecomponents.pdf, April 19th 1965
80. The 2024 NIMDZI 100,Nimdzi, https://www.nimdzi.com/nimdzi-100-top-lsp/, June 2024
81. AI and efficiency, Danny Hernandez, Tom Brown,OpenAI, https://openai.com/index/ai-and-efficiency/, 5 May 2020
82. Domain of notable artificial intelligence systems, by year of publication, Our World in Data, https://ourworldindata.org/grapher/domain-notable-artificial-intelligence-systems?facet=entity&uniformYAxis=1, 1 October 2024
83. Your Guide to Translation Cost Analysis in 2023, Smartling, https://www.smartling.com/resources/101/translation-rates/, 17 July 2023
84. Localization Pricing, Allcorect Game content studio, https://allcorrectgames.com/localization-pricing/, visited July 2024

85. English Letter Frequency Counts: Mayzner Revisited, Peter Norvig, , https://norvig.com/mayzner.html, 2013
86. Comparing Average Word Length Across Different Languages and Contexts, Gitnux, https://gitnux.org/average-word-length/, 17 July 2024
87. Video Game Voice Over Rates Unveiled, GoLocalise, https://golocalise.com/blog/video-game-voice-over-rates/, visited September 2024
88. AI Voice Cloning: Clone Your Voice in Minutes, ElevenLabs, https://elevenlabs.io/voice-cloning, visited September 2024
89. AI in organizations: Some tactics, Ethan Mollick, https://www.oneusefulthing.org/p/ai-in-organizations-some-tactics, 4 October 2024
90. AI Content on Steam, Valve, https://steamcommunity.com/groups/steamworks/announcements/detail/3862463747997849619, 9 January 2024
91. Video game performers strike over concerns about AI, Johny Walfisz, Euronews, https://www.euronews.com/culture/2024/07/26/video-game-performers-strike-over-concerns-about-ai, 26 July 2024
92. AI Clash Stalls Labor Talks for Video Game Actors, Producers, Ian Kullgren, Bloomberg Law, https://news.bloomberglaw.com/daily-labor-report/ai-clash-stalls-labor-talks-for-video-game-actors-producers, 29 August 2024
93. How the Use of AI Evolved Our Art Production Pipelines, Mario Toon, Mighty Bear, https://www.mightybeargames.com/post/how-the-use-of-ai-evolved-our-art-production-pipelines, 25 October 2023
94. Will We Run Out of Data? Limits of LLM Scaling Based on Human-Generated Data, Pablo Villalobos et al., Epoch AI, https://epochai.org/blog/will-we-run-out-of-data-limits-of-llm-scaling-based-on-human-generated-data, 6 June 2024
95. Dynabench: Rethinking Benchmarking in NLP, Douwe Kiela et al., NAACL 2021, https://arxiv.org/abs/2104.14337, 7 April 2021
96. Plotting Progress in AI, Douwe Kiela, https://contextual.ai/news/plotting-progress-in-ai/, 31 July 2023
97. Implications of connectivity and accessibility, Minnalearn, https://courses.minnalearn.com/en/courses/digital-revolution/the-internet-and-connectivity-revolution/the-implications-of-connectivity-and-accessibility/, visited 7 October 2024
98. Hugging Face, https://huggingface.co/huggingface, visited 7 October 2024
99. AI is replacing artists, and here's the proof, Paul Hatton, Creative Bloq, https://www.creativebloq.com/news/ai-is-taking-artists-jobs, 6 October 2023
100. Employer of new AI PhDs in the United States and Canada, Our World in Data, https://ourworldindata.org/grapher/employer-new-artificial-intelligence-phds-stacked-area, 28 June 2024
101. ChatGPT effect: Coursera sees signups for AI courses every minute in 2023, Divya Chowdhury et al., https://www.reuters.com/technology/chatgpt-effect-coursera-sees-signups-ai-courses-every-minute-2023-2024-01-18/, 18 January 2024
102. Coursera Inc (COUR) Q3 2024 Earnings Call Highlights: Solid Growth Amidst Challenges, GuruFocus News, yahoo!finance, https://finance.yahoo.com/news/coursera-inc-cour-q3-2024-072102889.html, 25 October 2024

103. Domain of notable artificial intelligence systems, by year of publication, Our World in Data, https://ourworldindata.org/grapher/domain-notable-artificial-intelligence-systems?facet=none, 1 October 2024
104. Share of artificial intelligence jobs among all job postings, Lightcast via AI Index, Our World in Data, https://ourworldindata.org/grapher/share-artificial-intelligence-job-postings, 8 June 2024
105. Global Artificial Intelligence Market Size (2024-2033), Market.us, https://market.us/report/artificial-intelligence-market/, September 2024
106. The global AI market is expected to reach $1.81 trillion by 2030, Faist, https://www.faistgroup.com/news/global-ai-market-2030/, 11 June 2024
107. Generative AI to Become a $1.3 Trillion Market by 2032, Research Finds, Mandeep Singh et al., Bloomberg, https://www.bloomberg.com/company/press/generative-ai-to-become-a-1-3-trillion-market-by-2032-research-finds/, 1 June 2024
108. Global Artificial Intelligence (AI) Market: Investments vs Potential, BCC Publishing, https://www.bccresearch.com/market-research/information-technology/artificial-intelligence-market-report.html, August 2024